Letters Home

By

Earle Kirkbride

iUniverse, Inc.
New York   Bloomington

Letters Home

iUniverse books may be ordered through booksellers or by contacting:

iUniverse
1663 Liberty Drive
Bloomington, IN 47403
www.iuniverse.com
1-800-Authors (1-800-288-4677)

Because of the dynamic nature of the Internet, any Web addresses or links contained in this book may have changed since publication and may no longer be valid. The views expressed in this work are solely those of the author and do not necessarily reflect the views of the publisher, and the publisher hereby disclaims any responsibility for them.

ISBN: 978-1-4401-3884-3 (pbk)
ISBN: 978-1-4401-3882-9 (cloth)
ISBN: 978-1-4401-3883-6 (ebk)

Printed in the United States of America

iUniverse rev. date: 05/20/2009

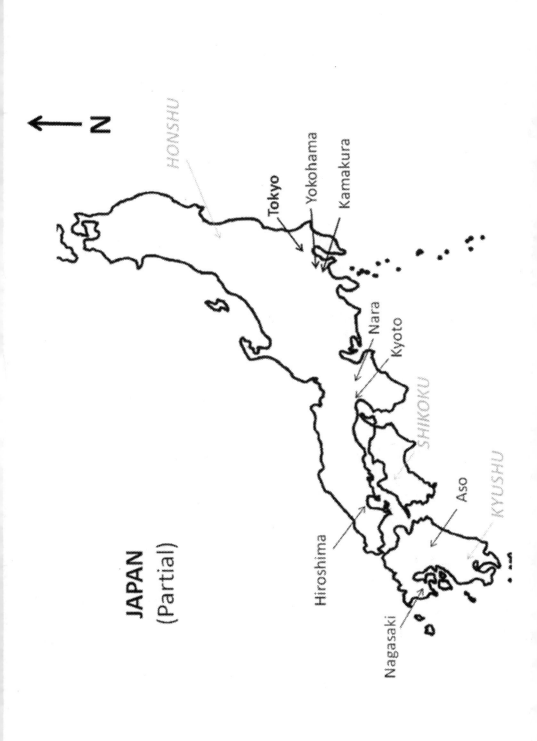

JAPAN
(Partial)

N

HONSHU

Tokyo

Yokohama

Kamakura

Nara

Kyoto

SHIKOKU

Aso

KYUSHU

Hiroshima

Nagasaki

To Jean
We did it!

Illustrations

Introduction

Norma Jean Cone was my late wife. During her lifetime, she told me stories about her work in Japan after WWII, and we discussed some day writing a book or screenplay about her experiences. We just never got around to it.

Last year, I discovered in my attic a box of letters from Jean to her family, starting in 1946. Her mother had saved them. It was like reading a diary. Although they are personal, I believe she would have been willing to share them, because they give a poignant perspective of what it was like for an American civilian woman to work and travel in devastated Japan right after WWII.

Her work was unusual. Attached to the 8th Army, she helped inventory the diamonds and precious metals worth many millions of dollars that were in vaults of the Bank of Japan in Tokyo. The inventory was classified Secret. At one time there were 250,000 karats of diamonds and precious stones. The vault also held one of the largest coin collections in the world, and vast hordes of gold, silver, and platinum. Just before Norma Jean arrived in Japan, the former Custodian of the Bank of Japan, Army Colonel Edward J. Murray, was arrested and court martialled for trying to smuggle over $200,000 worth of diamonds into the U.S.

It wasn't all work for an attractive, college graduate in the midst of 200,000 American soldiers. What to wear for the next dance sometimes became a problem. General Douglas MacArthur headed the occupying bureaucracy, as Supreme Commander for the Allied Powers (SCAP). The occupying Americans were living safely and well-cared-for in 1947 Japan. It is almost as if they lived in a comfortable cocoon. In *Letters Home* there are glimpses of how tough things were immediately after WW II for the Japanese, yet how hospitable they were to the American occupiers. One of the Army officers Jean was working with was glad to get back to Japan after a stateside visit, where things were "very hectic."

Jean's letters have 1940's slang expressions, and refer to product shortages continuing after World War II. For example, she was surprised that soap was available in the Post Exchange. Other letters regularly mention Nylon stockings. They were scarce. Also, initially she refers to "Japs" and "Nips". That is the way Americans referred to the Japanese during and immediately after WWII. The letters contain inconsistencies; they were written as personal communications with no thought that they would be published. For example, sometimes she spelled out ranks and numbers; other times she used numbers and abbreviations. Editing them would have reduced the personal nature of the letters, in my opinion.

The reader of *Letters Home* is also reminded of the differences between 1947 and the 21st Century in salaries, transportation, and communications. Her 1947 annual salary was less than $2,500, and the anticipated time by ship from New York to Yokahama was 52 days. It cost $12 for a three-minute appointment telephone call from Tokyo to Los Angeles.

Letters Home will entertain you as well as inform you about a facet of history few know about. You will view things through the eyes of an adventuresome young woman who worked and traveled in war-torn Japan and who even visited Korea as a rare American tourist just before North Korea invaded South Korea.

Earle Kirkbride

One

WESTERN
UNION

47 JAN 6
:S197 10=NEW YORK NY 6 824P
MR & MRS N J CONE=
:310 WEST LAUREL ST COMPTON CALIF=

SAILING FROM NEW YORK FRIDAY WILL CALL THURSDAY
NIGHT LOVE=
NORMA JEAN.

Thus, in 1947, began a two-year adventure for Norma Jean Cone, a twenty-three-year old UCLA graduate, as she headed for Japan— just 16 months after WWII ended with Japan's surrender. General Douglas MacArthur headed the occupation bureaucracy, as Supreme Commander for the Allied Powers (SCAP).

Leading up to the January departure for Japan was more than three months preparation in New York City. A California resident, she had been told New York was the best place to apply for overseas assignments with the federal government. Her parents had opposed her wish to join the armed forces during WWII, but they accepted her plans to go abroad as a civilian employee, rare as it was for young American women at that time.

During the three months in New York City, she took temporary office jobs and practiced typing to pass the Civil Service clerical test. Her letters from that period show the support she received from her family and the closeness she felt toward them. The letters also show how much she was enjoying New York. This joy of new experiences continues to be reflected in her letters from Japan.

The letters home often were playfully signed Jr., because her parents had planned to name her after her father had she been born a boy.

Oct. 13, 1946

Dearest Folks,

I am living at Kenmore Hall, which is located right off Lexington Ave. on 23rd St. Right across the street is N.Y. City College. It is a hotel, but the floor I'm on is exclusively for women. Most of them are girls working or going to school. I have a real comfortable bed with an innerspring mattress, chair, two lamps, bureau & an end table with drawers. It costs $10 per week. I'm not sure how long I can stay here. The Assistant Mgr. said indefinitely & yesterday the rm. clerk said only one week. I'm going to have another talk with the assis. mgr. this morning. I hope I can stay because it's such a wonderful location. A main subway station is only ½ block away & buses go up & down 23rd & Lexington.

I've talked to Ruth Troy a couple of times on the phone.[1] She hasn't been able to come over as the lady she works with is on her vacation, so Ruth has to work full time.

---

1   Ruth Troy was a cousin of her mother with overseas experience who was living in Philadelphia.

Monday I'm starting work in an office. It will be temporary as the woman at the USEES offices said there will be an opening in the State Hygiene Dept. soon that I may fill. So, I decided to work while I was waiting. I decided against the Airlines job, because it would be shift work & I didn't want to go out or come in alone at night.

Esther, you sound as busy as a sight-seer. It's never been as cold here as the night Esther left. The snow was only in upstate N.Y.

I got the check O.K. Mom. Thanks a million. My money is holding out O.K.

I got over my cold a couple of days after Esther left & have been well since. Even have gotten rid of my athletes foot. I bought some powder to put in my shoes & with that & Dr. Nichols ointment it all cleared up.

Must close & go see the assis. mgr. Write soon. Your letters are so wonderful, Mom.

Love,
Norma Jean

New address:
   145 E. 23rd St.
   N.Y.
P.S. The office (a toy co.) where I will work is only 3 blocks from here so I can walk to work.

October 14, 1946

Dearest Mom, Dad, & Esther,

I've just finished lunch & am planning on going swimming this afternoon. There's the nicest swimming pool & gym in the basement here. It is free to those who live here, so I've decided to practice up on my swimming. Will you please send me my bathing suit? It costs 10¢ to rent one, which is very cheap, but I'd rather have my own.

I went to the Federal Civil Service Commission to ask about that Jr. Prof. Assis. Test I took in 1945. They said they have quit giving appointments from that since last February. She referred me to the War Department to see what they might have. There they were taking applications for Overseas Civil Service Jobs. I inquired about those listed as Personnel Technician & Welfare Work. A lady interviewed me & said that since I had no military procedure experience I could not qualify. She suggested that if I want to, I could do general office work because of my experience at the Amer. Can Co. When I became experienced, she said, it would be possible to be promoted when I was there. The pay is good, $2442 a year. The Army provides housing at $15 mo. & meals cost about $1 a day. They also provide transportation to & from your destination. You sign up for a year. If you don't stay all that time, all that happens is that they won't pay for your return transportation. She wanted to give me a typing test right then, but I decided I'd have to practice first, as I knew I could never type the fifty words a minute. Also, I wanted to talk to somebody about it first.

I called Ruth Troy & explained the whole thing to her. The first thing she asked me was what you folks would think of it. I told her I didn't think they would object as we had talked of it before. She said it sounded good to her & thought it would be good experience for me. Soo—I rented a typewriter for $3 & have been practicing like mad. I am to let them know when I think I'm ready for the typing test, & they will time me.

I will start work tomorrow for the Turner Subscription Co. where I will do typing—for thirty dollars a week.

If I go overseas, it will probably be in the Pacific Theatre—Japan if possible. I'd just love to go. How does it sound to you? At the slow way my typing is coming I don't know when I'll be able to pass the test. Also, I will have to pass a physical exam & another interview.

The funniest thing happened. While I was waiting to be interviewed, I started talking to a woman about 60 years old. She said she had been a teacher in the Philippines for many years. I asked her if she knew Ervin Ross.[2] She said she did & asked about his wife. I said I didn't know anything about her, so she proceeded to tell me all she knew. It seems as though his wife's sister married a Pilipino in one of the Universities here. They went back to Manilla to live, but, because of

---

2   He was a distant cousin with whom she was to have considerable contact during future overseas assignments.

the race difference, were not accepted by either the whites or natives there. The sister sent for E's wife to come. She was living in some mid-western state. When she got there some of the white women told her the situation & warned her against marrying her brother-in-law's brother, as I guess her sister was planning for her. So E's wife stayed in the city & took a job with a drug Co. Not too long later Ervin married her. This lady said she was very pretty but was a lot younger than Ervin. They lived together for some time, then one day she left & never came back. That's as much as this lady knew & she often wondered about her as she thought E's wife was a very nice person. That's as far as we got, as my name was called.

Guess the Indian summer is all over here. It's quite chilly & windy. I'm sure glad I bought a wool dress, Esther. My coat is nice & warm, too. I wore them both to church yesterday & was comfortable all the time.

Two doors from me is the nicest Post Office. It's real big & modern. Even has guards who direct you around. I was in there this morning to send a clock back. I bought an alarm clock last week. When I went to wind it last night it wouldn't work. As it had a 90-day guarantee I sent it right back this morning.

Will you please send this letter to Larry?[3] I know I need the typing practice but think I do better on straight copy & screwy sentences like "The brown fox jumped over the little lazy dog".

The maid wants to clean my room & I want to go swimming so will close for now. Oh yes, guess I can stay here indefinitely 'cause when I asked the Assis. Mgr. about it he said "Don't worry"—the room clerk was standing there, too.

I'd like to know what you think of my overseas plans. There's still a lot of tests to be passed before I could go.

Love to all,
Norma Jean

---

3   Larry was her brother.

October 21, 1946
Mon. eve.

Dearest Mom,

Just a note before I go to bed. I received your wonderful letter today. It was so good to hear all the local news. I was especially glad to get it, as I walked home (7 blocks each way) on my lunch hour. I just had a hunch I'd have a letter waiting for me—yours was it!

I've just been visiting with the girl next to me. Her name is Evelyn, & she works in an office near by. I explained to her why I was doing so much typing. She said she thought I must be writing a book. The reason I'm not typing this letter is it's too late, & I'm afraid I'd have the other neighbors on my neck.

Saturday, I went to the Music Hall Theatre & saw

"The Jolson Story". It was good. The stage show was just wonderful—never seen such beautiful scenery & costumes in my life. It's entirely different from the one we saw, Esther. This one's theme is United Nations.

Hope I hear from Larry soon. In the last letter I got from him, he said not to write until he gives me his new address. I suppose it's on the way.

How's the food situation there? We are getting a little more meat here now. The paper says sugar will be in the stores by the end of next week.[4]

It rained today, but it is not cold. I haven't been in swimming since I got my bathing suit, but Evelyn & I are planning to go soon. She went tonight, but I decided to practice some more.

The little iron sure is nice. I do all my own slips, blouses, etc. with it. Even used it to keep my feet warm one night, & it really did.

I wish you all the luck in the world on your Civil Service Test, Esther. I'm betting on you coming out on top.

Must close as I'm sooo sleepy. Thanks again for your wonderful letter, Mom—it was worth every step of the walk home & more. Goodnight, dearies.

Love,
Norma Jean

---

4   This is an example of the shortages that still existed for Americans immediately after WWII.

October 25, 1946

Dearest Esther, Mom, & Dad,

I just got home from work & received the package with my bathing suit & the Compton paper. Thanks a lot for both. Also, I got the UCLA Magazine & your good letters. I'm going to look Verna Mae Stroh up that you marked in the Mag. as I knew her at CJC & UCLA.[5]

Thanks for the stamps, Esther-Mae.

I keep so busy I don't have time to do half the things I want to do. As you've probably been reading, the United Nations is meeting here in NYC. Every night they have programs in Rockefeller Center. I went to the one last night & am going again tonight. Last night was folk dances of Britain, Scotland, Poland, & Norway. The costumes were so pretty. It is held where they ice skate. It is free admission & everyone stands around the edge. The weather was just perfect last night—clear & just cool enough to be comfortable with a coat on. Also, last night was a speaker from the Gt. Britain Delegation. Tonight, they are going to have more folk dancing, choral music, & a speaker. It lasts for about 1½ hrs.

I have fun at work. Every noon, two girls (Frances & Rita) & I go to lunch together. They've taken me to all the different restaurants that they know are good. It's sure fun. One day we had hot Pastrami sandwiches (like corned beef) at a delicatessen. Everyone puts catsup on their fries & tips the waitress a nickel there. Yesterday, we went to a little Italian restaurant downstairs. We had Ravioli & Tortoni (rum flavored ice cream) for dessert. The Starlight Cafe is our favorite though. You get a full dinner for 60¢ here & it's very good.

You're certainly going to have a houseful of people. Bet you'll have fun though. I'd like to drop in & see everyone.

Would you mind sending me the article on orient jobs, Mom? I'd like to read it very much. I took a timed typing test at the YW the other night. I did all right on that so will soon take the Civil Service Test. My speed is all right now, but I still make more mistakes than I should. You should see me at work—the girl next to me has typed for years & is a whiz. Next to her it sounds as though I'm just playing around.

---

5   Compton Junior College.

I got a nice letter from Ruth Troy day before yesterday. She & Jack are going to Wash. D.C. for a Navy Day celebration. She's still working everyday.

I like my place where I'm staying. I can have it indefinitely. Sure was lucky in getting in. They say the leaves have turned very nicely now in the country so am going to try to go out a ways this Sunday to see them.

Do you want those pictures back, Esther?

I must close so I can go & get a good place to see the show at Rockefeller Center. Got to beat all the old ladies to the good seats.

Love,

Norma Jean

PS Have you seen or heard from Yvonne lately? How are Margaret & Frances?

It's all right with me if Ione & Bud use my UCLA tickets. My membership is all paid up for this year, so be sure to use my name for anything you want that may come to me from them through the mail.

I hope you're all over your cold Dad. Everyone here is having them too.

Nov. 6, 1946

Dearest Mom, Dad, Esther, & Aunt Kate,

Was so glad to receive your wonderful letter, Dad. I'm glad you spent Halloween that way!

I think I'm about the happiest person in New York tonight. I took the typing test today & passed. Still don't know how I did it 'cause I was so excited. They first told me I was scheduled to leave for duty in Tokyo, Japan. That's all I could think of when I took the test. My lucky stars were with me, & I typed 53 words a minute. Next, they sent me down to have a physical. It lasted about 2 hours, & boy was it thorough. Guess I passed it too, for at the end, they gave me shots for typhoid, smallpox, tetanus, & diphtheria. It says on a paper I have that they give you the inoculations only if you are found physically qualified. I was talking to some of the other girls there, & they said it usually takes about 6 weeks for processing (meaning more shots) before you can leave. If that's so, I'll probably leave just before Christmas. The other girls were either going to Tokyo or Frankfurt, Germany. As it was election day here in New York, our office was closed, which was another lucky break for me, as I won't lose the days pay. I have to go back to the Army Dispensary once a week though from now on for my shots & in between, if my arms get red.

I didn't go to Uncle Albert's last week-end. Just as I was leaving, I happened to ask for my mail, & they gave me the letter telling of the test. I decided I'd better stay here & practice & rest. I was really disappointed 'cause I had been planning all week on going. I called them & told them I was not coming. They said they were disappointed too, but it would be best if I came another week-end.

How's California, Aunt Kate? Wish I could just drop in for an evening or so & have a good visit with all of you.

Must close, as I'd like to go down to Times Square & see the election excitement.

Hope you have just as much luck on your Civil Service Test, Esther, as I had on mine—will be thinking of you.

Lots of love to all,
Norma Jean

Nov. 6, 1946

Dearest Folks,

Just a quickie before I go to bed. I had another interview at the War Dept. this morning. They said I would sail from Seattle, Wash., but don't know when. They have to send the reams of forms I signed to Wash. D.C., then wait for a port call. I can take 400 pounds of baggage. My expenses will be paid to Seattle on the train. I can take two suitcases with me in the stateroom, & the rest will go in the ship's hold.

I was given a checklist of things to bring. Also, she said that she had no complaints from the people she has sent to Tokyo, & they seem to like it there. From Europe, however, she said she has been receiving numerous complaints.

That article you sent sure helps, Mom. I sure have a lot of work ahead of me in getting everything organized.

The interviewer also said that as of Oct. 1ˢᵗ, all overseas personnel had to sign for two years service abroad. I was surprised because they told me one year before—anyhoo it's two years now.

I'm supposed to take a two-year's supply of clothes with me but decided I didn't have the time or money for all that. Maybe, those super shoppers Esther & Mom could send me some as I need them, Hmm?

Got your swell letter, too, Mom. Just love to hear that local news.

Got a new girl friend. Her name is Primrose Milligan. She is real cute. I thought by her accent that she was English, but she's straight from Scotland. Has only been in this country about a month. She lives right across the hall from me. She & Evelyn & I are always popping in and out of each other's rooms. Tonight, we ate at Prexys who serve "Hamburgers With a College Education."

You'd better come to N.Y. to get warm. Last week, we really had an Indian Summer. Tonight, it's chilly in the wind but warm inside. I'm so tired I'm groggy so must close.

Love,
N.J., Jr.

November 12, 1946

Dearest Folks,

Received your super letter, yesterday, Mom & the one from Bobbie enclosed—got them on my lunch hour.

Today, I had more shots for Typhus & Typhoid. Friday, I go for Diphtheria & next Tuesday for more Typhoid & Typhus & I think

Tetanus. My arms are a little sore again tonight, but that will go away in a couple of days. They are just great to me at the office, about letting me have time off to get them. I explained it all to them from the first, & they told me to take off whenever I have to, & I don't have to make up the time. They asked me to work there as long as I could.

I'm thinking about Esther & her exam this week. Wish you the best, kiddo.

I'd love to see your bedroom, Mom. The color combinations sound perfect. I'm not promising anything, but I'm going to try to get to California before I leave. I'm going to try to be all ready when my port call comes through, so I can leave immediately. This will give me a few extra days, I believe, as they usually give you a few days to get ready in after the call. As long as I'm at Seattle I'd love to go to Spokane, but, as yet, haven't figured out how I can swing it.[6] I plan to go see them at the War Dept. again & see if they can tell me if I can plan some stopovers on my trip. Might as well get their money's worth. I will get pay for food on the trip, too. I think she said $6 a day on the train.

Speaking of money, I have some urgent business to take up with some of you. As I won't get my travel pay until after I arrive in Tokyo, I will have to pay for all of it first myself. With clothes, trunk, etc. I'll have to buy, I won't be able to manage it all on my bank account, that's for sure. Sooo—honeybunches, sweetie pies, darlings, & moneybags, I've thought of a plan. If you don't like it just tell me, & any suggestions will be gladly received. How about my borrowing as much money as I think I'll need from one of you? Then, when I get my travel pay over there, I can return it. Also, I can make an allotment to someone. I think I'd like to make this out to the one I borrow the money from as it would be an easy & sure way of paying you back & also would save confusion when I wanted you to buy & send things to me. I thought it might be best to borrow it from Esther or Dad, as I realize it would be more convenient for them to meet banking or postal saving hours than Mom. The only thing is, I think it would be less confusing if I just borrowed it from one person, don't you think?

The only thing I've bought so far for my trip is a tube of lipstick. I have been shopping around & pricing other things, however. A trunk, which I'll need, runs around $35 at most stores. I have another

---

6   She was born in Spokane and had relatives there.

problem. The little book says "You will enjoy a small radio if you can bring one. They are exorbitant in price here (Japan) & hard to find. The electric current in Japan is usually 100 volts & 50 cycles. Any good AC radio should be satisfactory on the low voltage. Bring extra tubes. None are available here." How is my little one working? I don't know if I should try to take it or not, as I'd like to pack it in the trunk here in N.Y., or else it will count as another piece of luggage & we're only allowed to have two pieces with us on the ship. I was looking at radios in a store here & spotted a small one, which is also short wave. The salesman said I could get the U.S. on it but with a regular radio I would only get local Jap stations. The price on it is $29.10. Do you have any ideas on this subject? I do want to take a radio with me.

I was sure glad I had a wallet-sized birth certificate made, as it saved me a trip back to the War Dept. last week. The girl was sure surprised. She asked me to bring it in to her the next morning, & I came right back with "I have it with me."

I have still another problem—Christmas cards. I'm trying to get them taken care of now to be ready for anything later. The thing that has me stumped is the people in Kansas. What are you doing about that, Esther? I'm not sending them to the other relatives. Thought I'd rather put my time & money on cards to people from Japan, if I ever get there.

I'm going to continue looking at & pricing things for awhile, & I won't buy them until I'm more positive of my plans.

This has turned out to be a problem letter. I'd give a lot for an evening's talk with you to help me. I'd also give a lot to have you go shopping with me—you know how I get in stores! I'll appreciate your being "Frank" & "Ernest" on any of these matters.[7]

Must close for now.

Love, N.J. Jr.

---

7   Refers to characters in a popular comic strip.

Nov. 21, 1946

Darling Esther,

Your "Quickie" was a goodie. Was surely surprised to see all the green stuff. I don't know how I'll ever be able to thank you enough. I'm the luckiest kid in the world for having such a wonderful sister. Gosh, I'd give anything if you could only be going with me. I'll work & save my money in Tokyo, & at the end of my stay there, maybe we can plan for you to meet me part way (like Hawaii), & we can do more sightseeing, eh kiddo?

I really don't think I'll need any more money, as I still have $150 of my own in the bank & with Mom's $50 I'm pretty well set. I bought the radio & am enjoying it. Tonight, I bought Navy blue wool slacks & a Navy blue wool cardigan sweater. The only big things I'll have to buy yet are a dark suit, black dress, & trunk, so with your money I will be able to manage fine.

I got a letter from Jill. I had written telling her of my Japan plans. She was so enthusiastic for me & wants me to come to Spokane if possible.

It still hasn't gotten very cold here. A few days were very cool, but it is warm tonight & feels like rain.

I'd better make this a quickie too & run along to bed. Thanks again for your morale & financial support.

Oceans of love to my angel sister.

Norma Jean

11-24-46

Dearest Folks,

Just a line before bed--the announcer just said "Good Morning," so it's after midnight. Had a quiet week-end. Did some shopping Sat. Went to church & then saw "Razors Edge" today. Am enjoying my radio so much.

Love,
N.J., Jr.

Nov. 26, 1946
Tues. Evening

Dearest Folks,

"Ah, yes, there's good news tonight". I got a letter from the War Dept. today as follows:

"Rec'd Travel Orders for you. This office (N.Y.) is now awaiting a port call. Please do not call this office, as you will be notified immediately when a port call is received."

That's all I know, but think I'd better have everything ready for action anytime now. I'm really going to do some shopping Sat. I'll send a Special Delivery or wire you when I find out when I am to leave. Still can't believe it's actually going to be so soon, but the sooner the better, as I'm getting so anxious now.

My radio is perfect. It is a Crosley Short Wave & plays beautifully. I first had a Pilot radio but didn't like it as it had too much static. I took it back & got this one. It cost $30.55 tax & all. It is white plastic & small enough to pack in my trunk. It has a built in aerial & is specially made for short wave receiving, so I will be able to get the States from there.

I wish I could take Kenmore Hall with me. It's really swell here. I'm getting to know a lot of the people around. Went swimming last night with my bloody buddy swimming teachers. The Assistant Mgr. is so nice to me & keeps asking about my Japan trip. Last week, they gave us all clean bedspreads & drapes that match. Mine is green & pink floral creton (sp) & the spread has a flounce all around it.

Tonight, Betty Brown & I had dinner together. She's from Texas. She said I was the first person she's really visited with since she's hit N.Y. two weeks ago & believe me she really made up for those two silent weeks. Ya-ta-ta, ya-ta-ta!! She just landed a job as an accountant & will start at $225 a month.

Golly Moses, the announcer said "good morning." I must close as I still have to put up my hair & get things ready to go to Philadelphia tomorrow right after work. Got a nice letter from Larry. More later.

Love, Norma Jean

P.S. I thought the "Razors Edge" was wonderful. Don't miss it.

Nov. 29, 1946

Dearest Mom, Dad, Esther, & Aunt Kate,

I received your wonderful letter this morning before I went to work, Esther, & enjoyed it so very much. Your suggestions are really helping me. I think I will get a formal skirt & blouses tomorrow.

I went to Wanamaker's tonight & got underthings (longies, too), wool gloves, blouses (white), & a trunk. The trunk was really a bargain. They had them advertised, & I got the last one they had. Tax & all it was only $24.34. The couple who bought one just before me were from the Norwegian Diplomatic Service & could scarcely speak English. He showed his passport & didn't have to pay the Fed. Tax. The store will deliver it Wednesday here at Kenmore.

I bought a dress from Ruth Troy yesterday. She bought it then decided she didn't like it, 'cause it was too young for her. I think it's real cute. It's asparagus soup green wool, push-up sleeves, bow tie neckline, gold buttons to the waist, full skirt, plain waist. It fits perfectly, & the length is just right, too. She paid $16.95 for it & would only let me give her $10 for it. Better not mention it in your letter to them, as Jack never knew she bought the dress & would only make a fuss &

might scold Ruth. I'm real tickled with it & Ruth said she's happy too, because she never felt good in it.

I'm enclosing my Alumni Assoc. card, as it may help you in getting tickets. Keep it as long as you want, but when you're through send it back. Before the war, they had a Bruin Club in Tokyo, so maybe they will again. Anyway, it will be several months before I'll want it. I'd suggest you call U.C.L.A. (Arizona 30971) right away & ask them how to get tickets. Ask for the Alum. Assoc. Office. Just tell them you're me, as it'd be less confusing. If you want to write to them, I see their address is on the back of the card. Sure hope you can get some. Larry said he heard Alumni couldn't get any, but I think you can. I heard over the radio that they will probably play Illinois. Everyone here thinks Army got gypped by not getting to go. U.C.L.A. is really well known here—much more than U.S.C. Am really glad I can say I went there.

Must close & go to bed so that I can be fresh for tomorrow's shopping tour. I am checking things off my list pretty good now. Hope to have everything bought & packed by next weekend, so I can be ready to leave at a moment's notice. I'm trying not to count on Calif. too much, as I might be so disappointed. I'll try my best & see how things turn out.

Feel like I've written a sequel to "Gone With the Wind." My correspondence is terrific—still haven't answered lots of letters.

All my love to my favorite people,
Norma Margaret Mitchell Jean

Nov. 30, 1946

Dearest Dad,

I was overwhelmed to open your letter & find such a wonderful surprise. The card is so nice. I have it Scotch taped on the wall where I can see it best. I don't know how I can thank you for your generosity on the money order. All I can say is a million thanks, Dad.

I went shopping again today. I'm wearing the slack suit I bought, & it is very comfortable. It is teal blue, pin-stripe corduroy. It fits perfectly. It is very tailored with a long jacket. Ordinarily, I don't care for corduroy, but this is such a wonderful quality that it looks very good. It will be nice & warm, too. I also got a pair of shoes, which are really my pride & joy. They are the most comfortable things I've ever had on. The leather is soft kid. I saw a pair like them in a window in New Haven. I asked where they sold that brand here & was told McCreery's had them. I got the last pair in my size. I wish Esther could get a pair, as I think they'd look good on her & be real comfortable. Tell her to ask to see Gold Cross "Cobbie Casuals" #23421. The ceiling price on them is $8.95 too.[8]

I found the best place to eat tonight. A lady recommended it to me. The food is just like a home-cooked meal. The dinner was only 85¢ & included soup, salad, pot roast & gravy, string beans, mashed turnips, candied yams, bread & biscuits, butter, coffee, & dessert (I chose fruit cup.)

The only way the coal strike has affected N.Y. yet is the dim-out at night.[9] It sure is a lot darker. I almost didn't get off the bus at my stop the first night, because all my light landmarks were missing. I have steam heat in my room, & it is always comfortably warm.

Well, Pop, I better sign off for now. I still think I'm the luckiest person in the world. I wouldn't trade being N.J., Jr. for anything. I'm going to buy something extra special; I think it will be Aphrodesia perfume with the money for myself on Dec. 7.[10] Consider your

---

8   "Ceiling" prices were established during WWII.

9   There were two strikes by bituminous coal miners in 1946. The first started April 1st and was ended by President Truman taking over the mines in mid May. The second started November 21st and ended December 7th.

10 Her birthday.

Christmas shopping for me done too, Dad, because this is enough for lots of Holidays.

Thanks again for remembering me.

All my love,
Norma Jean

Dec. 2, 1946

Dearest Folks,

Just got through putting away the things you sent me. The assortment was just wonderful. I was so happy to see my good old T-shirt that I put it on & am still wearing it. I've tried on my formal & the shoes—just like seeing old friends. Thanks for the nylons; they're lovely. The box of hankies was such a cute surprise. A million thanks for all your thoughtfulness & efforts.

Yesterday, I went to Flushing Meadows to see the United Nations buildings. I saw the main lounge, general assembly hall, future UN building exhibition, restaurant, & ate at the cafeteria. It is all very modern & spic & span. Marines in full dress are guards. I want to reserve tickets & see them in session at Lake Success next. I've got the phone number. You can't call sooner than 24 hours before you want the tickets.

My poor little old room is getting so crammed with boxes, clothes, shoes, etc. I'll soon have to move out & let them have it. My trunk is to be delivered Wednesday. So far, I can't see where I'll have room to put the chair then. I'm going to pack the trunk, then store it in the basement until I get my call.

Must close so I can clear my way to bed. Thanks again for your wonderful packing job. I'm so pleased with everything you included. By the way, my formal really looks sharp with the black choker & earrings I have. 'Bye for now.

Love,
Norma Jean

P.S. How are the Rose Bowl tickets coming?

I just heard over the news that the U.N. will probably be permanently situated in San Francisco. Don't blame 'em after these icy blasts.

Dec. 8, 1946

Dearest Mom,

Received your wonderful letter & package Dec. 6. The stockings are lovely—never have I had so many nice ones all at once. I just love the diary & it's just what I wanted. Almost bought myself one last week but am so glad I waited. It wasn't half as nice as this one. The card is just darling. I have all my cards from Dad, you, Esther, Larry & Jill on the wall.

I bought a black evening skirt yesterday. It's black crepe with fullness in the front. I had to get size 18 in order for it to be long enough. They are altering the waist line for me & will send it out. I looked but have not spotted any sharp blouses yet.

Starting Mon. the stores will be open every evening until Christmas. There were really rib-crushing crowds in town Saturday. The decorations are just beautiful in the stores. At 34th & Broadway, Gimbels, Macy's & Saks got together & all decorated their stores alike. They have huge peppermint sticks with green wreaths.

The weather isn't as cold as it was. I'm still hoping for snow before I leave.

I'm glad the Rose Bowl tickets came through. I will answer Esther's nice letter real soon. Are those new shots helping her?

I'd better close for now, as I want to take a shower & go to bed early. Thanks loads & loads for your letter & presents. It certainly is a wonderful feeling to know you're all behind me.

Goodnight, darling Mother.

Love,
Norma Jean

Mon. morning Dec. 9

I felt pretty weak this morning so didn't go to work. Have just finished breakfast here at the hotel. Received a birthday card from Clarise & the package of soap Esther sent from Faye. Friends is good.

Dec. 9, 1946

Dearest Esther,

Just a note tonight to thank you for the darling birthday card. Gee, I was so well remembered on Dec. 7. Larry sent me a awfully cute one, too. I finished the cookies you sent on Dec. 7 & enjoyed them to the last crumb. The soap from Faye arrived this morning also. I think that was so sweet of her to remember me. Will you please send me her address, as I'd like to write her a thank you note.

Your idea about waiting for my shipping orders in California is a good one, but I doubt if it could be worked. I still have to get more shots from the Army here. I'll talk to them at the War Dept. again & see what they say. Also, it would foul my transportation up, as they make all the baggage arrangements for you from here.

Have the Rose Bowl tickets come? As long as I can't go I'll be so happy knowing you'll be right in there pitching for the blue & gold. Only wish you could have gotten more tickets.

I've enjoyed my radio so much these past few days when I've not been feeling so hot. Right now, they're playing songs from "Carousel" ("You'll Never Walk Alone Now"). It sure reminds me of that rainy day when we saw it together. Weren't we a mess? But, wasn't it fun?

Must close for this evening & go back to bed. I'm feeling better & plan on going back to work tomorrow. I realize how terribly busy you are at this time of the year & doubly appreciate all of your letters & those luscious cookies. I sincerely hope this finds you well & not in too much of a frazzle. I want you to be in good shape for that meeting in Tokyo, kiddo.

All my love,
Norma Jean

December 15, 1946

Dearest Larry,

What a wonderful surprise to receive your gift. I just love it. It is the nicest one I've seen. I really needed it too, as my old UCLA wallet is getting worn out. The colors in this one are perfect, as it will be easy to find in a black purse. It will be grand for traveling—especially with that hideaway pocket so all my $100 bills (ha!) won't show. You have the best taste, Larry. Many, many thanks.

It is Sunday evening, & I have just finished listening to Jack Benny, Fred Allen, etc. Earlier, I went to church then when it got dark went to Rockefeller Plaza to see the Christmas tree. It's immense. I heard over the radio it was 75 ft. high. The lighting at night makes it look purplish-blue. It has many different colored, large lights strung about it topped with a huge silver star. Ice skating goes on as usual in the Plaza, as the tree is set above the ice floor at the far end.

I enclosing the program I got yesterday at Flushing Meadows. Three other girls & I got tickets for the 4 o'clock session. It was very interesting. The interpreting system surprised me though. Everything had to be said twice. If the speaker spoke in English, an interpreter got up at the conclusion of the speech & translated into French & vice-versa, if the speaker spoke in French. They were having a debate about the non-self-governing territories. We heard delegates from the U.S., England, France, India, & China. The one from India was by far the best orator. He got a hearty applause from the public section. It was hard to get too much out of it all, as they kept getting into legalities of the wording of the UN Charter. We ate our dinner in the cafeteria there.

Another interesting thing was the television sets they had in the public lounge. You could sit there & see what was going on inside. You could really see the speaker better this way, as the public section is at the back of the auditorium. Would you please send the program home when you're finished with it, as I'd like the folks to see it, & I just got one.

Still haven't heard anything further from my Japan deal but am ready to go anytime.

How's school? Are you still working? I know you must be terribly busy.

I'm tired so must turn in myself. Thanks again for the lovely pocketbook—nothing could have pleased me more. 'Bye for now.

Love,
Norma Jean

P.S. The little birthday gift card is just darling, too.

Dec. 19, 1946

Dearest Mom, Dad, Esther, Larry, & Aunt Kate,

I received the package today. I've fixed my room all up tonight & it looks so cute with the little Christmas tree & all. I have all the packages arranged around the tree, corsage & candy stick on the end table. Above it, I am Scotch taping the Christmas cards on the wall.

Your Christmas card was just darling, Mom & Dad. I also enjoyed those pictures so much. I had been wishing I had a picture by which to show off my wonderful family to friends. I do wish I had one that included Larry too, as I have none of him.

I went down town tonight to look for a navy skirt. My old one is almost shot & I wanted one for my red jerkin. I came home with a navy suit. It is so nice as it's just what I need. It's wool gabardine, cardigan style. It's tailored just beautifully & fits perfectly with no needed alterations. I got it at Franklin-Simon on Fifth Ave. & it cost $35. It will be wonderful to travel in. Franklin-Simon & McCreery's are my favorite stores here.

There are so many things I want to do. The big churches are all having Christmas programs now that I want to take in. Also, I'm watching for when they turn the lights on the big Christmas trees on Park Ave.

Sat. morning I'm planning on going to the Radio City Music Hall Theatre to see "Till the Clouds Roll By," and take in their famous Christmas stage show. Esther Mae, you can bet I'll see the stage show twice—remember how we did? This may be the last Christmas I'll spend in New York so am really going to try to see everything—the weekends are so short though.

Time to turn in for tonight. Good night for now dearies. Will try to be a good li'l kid & wait to open those interesting looking packages.

Love,
Norma Jean

Dec. 26, 1946

Dearest Mom, Dad, Larry, Esther, & Aunt Kate,

In my mail box just now was a special delivery letter from the War Dept. as follows: "A port call has been received for you for Jan. 7, 1947 through the New York Port of Embarkation. It is requested that you report to this office at your own expense 6 Jan. at 9:30 a.m. for necessary information."

So that's where I stand. Gee, I'm excited all over again.

Esther, nothing could have pleased me more than that picture you sent. I think it is very good of you. I was so excited when I got it, I went to everybody I know in K. H. & showed it off. The coloring is so good, & the frame is just darling. A million thanks for everything—only hope I can be half as wonderful a sister to you as you've been to me. You think of everything, kiddo.

Mom & Dad, thanks for everything you've done to make my Christmas as near perfect as it could be away from home. I wore the corsage you sent to our office party. With the money you sent, Dad, so far I've bought Aphodesia perfume & a strapless bra—both things I've wanted so badly but hated to splurge on.

Guess what! I saw it snow! It happened last Thurs. I got so excited I could scarcely work. All the kids at work got tickled at me 'cause I could hardly take my eyes off the windows. I really felt full-fledged when I got hit by a snowball on the way home that night. I liked the snow so much I couldn't stay in, so I walked all over town. The stores & streets were deserted as most people stayed home because of the storm, but I loved it.

Saturday, I went to the Music Hall Theatre & saw "Til the Clouds Roll By" & their stage show. All I can say is it's just out of this world. I wished & wished all of you could have been there with me. Yep, I saw the stage show twice & would have enjoyed it the third time but could sit no longer. Sunday, I went to Christ M.E. Church on Park Ave. in the a.m. I always enjoy it there so much as the service is just like at home; the church is beautiful & the people are nice. The ushers always wear black cut-away coats with striped trousers & grey gloves. In the afternoon, I went to the candlelight carol service at Riverside Church. It is the Baptist one Rockefeller built. It is over twenty floors high. The music was beautiful & the candlelight service was so impressive.

Monday night, Evelyn came over for our special celebration. She had tickets to a party given by her brother's boss. It was close, so we went. They had a buffet supper, entertainment on the stage & dancing. We came home about 11 o'clock & then I opened my gifts from home. Her home is here in N.Y. She's really a pal.

Tuesday, we quit work at 3:30 for our party. We exchanged 50 cent gifts. I gave stationery & got a cute little plastic dog. The firm gave us each $10, a box of French chocolates, & furnished sandwiches, wine, & cookies for our party. They are all so nice to me. I got several Christmas cards from the girls there too.

Here it is after 2 a.m. already. I could go on for hours. Oh, for a real visit with you to get this all hashed out. Am anxious to hear about your Christmas too. Am still so excited about the past, present, & future that I'm not sleepy, but I'd better relax & go to bed. I'm so happy. Never thought so many of my wishes could come true. With such a wonderful family & relatives behind me I feel I have a lot to live up to.

Thanks to each one of you for everything. Will continue this soon as there's much more to be told. 'Bye now & Happy New Year.

All my love,
Norma Jean

Dec. 27, 1946

Dearest Folks,

Have just gotten home from an evening with Katherine Cullmer. She met me here at Kenmore Hall at 5:30. We had dinner together in K.H.'s new Baguette Room dining room. It is real cute—quilted walls & ceiling in blue & lots of mirrors with soft music—atmosphere all over the place. Anyway—we had a nice dinner. Katherine fell in love with Kenmore Hall & says she'd like to spend her vacation here. After dinner, we went to her house in Brooklyn & she showed me through it. Dick & I had a nice visit. Then she took me to her friend Pat's house. She served us cider, fruit cake & candy. Katherine & Pat drove me back to K.H. & Katherine showed Pat all around so enthusiastically. I showed them my Christmas gifts, read them their horoscopes from my diary & fed them candy. They just left & it's 12:30. I sure like Katherine. I think she's more excited about my trip than I am. She sure appreciated your card & note, Esther. She showed it to me tonight. She's going to come to see me again before I go.

Am quitting work next week, so I can get everything ship-shape & get a little extra rest. I have loads of letters to write & am planning on spending this weekend doing it. Also have to have another inoculation next Friday.

According to the radio, we're in for snow tomorrow. If so, am planning to ride to Central Park, as they say it is so pretty in the snow.

I have been looking over my finances just now and decided I'd better speak to my banker pronto. As it is, I don't have enough in case I should get a chance to fly home. Would it be possible for me to have about $200, as then I would have plenty.

I'd rather have it & not need it then need it & not have it. Guess I'll be leaving Jan. 7 so would like the money by then if possible.

I meant to tell you before that if any of the things I sent you don't fit or were broken, send them right back, as I saved all the receipts. I had six pictures taken at Wanamaker's. I never like my own pictures. As usual, I couldn't decide how to wear my hair so compromised by having two poses. I like the one with it down best but sent both to you just for laughs.

Must close for tonight as I've a million things to do tomorrow.

Love,
Norma Jean

P.S. Just received your nice Christmas letters. Was so glad to hear about your Christmas.

The weatherman was wrong. It's a beautiful, clear, sunny day.

Love,
N.J. Jr.

Dec. 29, 1946

Dearest Folks,

It's Sunday evening & I'm just winding up a quiet weekend. It was rainy & stormy today, so I decided to stay in & write letters, wash, iron, & pack.

Betty Brown came about four o'clock; we talked 'til about six then had dinner together & she went home. We ate at a cute new restaurant near Grand Central Station called "Glorified Ham'n Eggs." They serve them right in the skillets they're cooked in. It opened last night at 12 o'clock, so we really got in on their debut. It was sure good. I had ham & eggs & Betty had a Western Omelet.

This is the fourteenth letter I've written this weekend, so if I repeat something I've already told you, it'll be no wonder.

Yesterday, Saturday, I suddenly decided I'd have to see Helen Hayes in the play "Happy Birthday" before I left. I got to the box office at about one o'clock. Natch, no more seats were available for the 2:40 show, but they said there was standing room ($1.80) for the later show. I latched on to one of those tickets & spent up until show time writing letters on the corner at the Astor Hotel. It wasn't bad standing at all. They had padded rails to lean on right behind the orchestra seats. I sat down during intermission & never did get too tired. I'm so glad I went as Helen Hayes was wonderful. She's so tiny. This is the first play that she's sang & danced in. One of the highlights was when she dove from on top of the bar & was caught by two men just before she hit the floor. It was a comedy & really funny. Will send the program home with a bunch of other junk next week.

New Year's Eve, I will just have to see Times Square, although they say you practically get torn to shreds.

I got another evening blouse yesterday. It is black satin with a black lace inset running diagonally across the front. It has a round neck, cap sleeves, a peplum with a bow on the side front, & black jet buttons down the back. It really looks like a black one-piece gown with my skirt. Think I'll get long black gloves to go with it. It cost $10.95 at Burnetts, which I thought was a real bargain. I don't think I told you about the other blouse I got. It is white crepe, very plain with cap sleeves & has several rows of black trimming around the round neck line. Sure wish I could show you all these things.

Unless the weatherman is wrong again, we're in for "snow, sleet, & sub-zero weather." Guess I'm just warm blooded, because everyone's been complaining about the cold, but I haven't felt it at all. Betty said she's been cold ever since she landed here from Texas. But then, she's as thin as Olive Oyl & you know me—wasting away to a mere ton.[11]

Must close & do my ironing. The clothes dry in a jiffy with this steam heat. Don't know how I ever got along without those blue slippers as I wear them constantly.

'Bye now

Love,

Norma Jean

---

11 A character in the Popeye cartoon series.

Jan. 2, 1947

Dearest Esther,

Congratulations! I was so happy & proud of your passing the Civil Service Exam with such flying colors. I'd sure been wondering about it. I don't think you're stuck in a rut but really playing the fox. Jobs like that are few & far between—you should see what college grads are working for here.[12] I'm so happy for you.

Received your special delivery yesterday (New Years Day). Thanks a million for the money. Now, I'm ready, come Hell or high water.

I had a nice New Years Day. I met Betty Brown & we heard noon mass at St. Patricks. The church was packed. She insisted we sit in the very front row, so I really had a ringside seat. The church is beautiful now with loads of poinsettias & red & white candles. She said her relatives in the Bronx had invited me to come with her to dinner, so I went. We had a wonderful roast beef dinner & later we had supper. Home cooking tastes so good. They were so nice to me—guess I just naturally have a hungry look 'cause they kept feeding me candy, cookies, etc. all afternoon. It was Betty's cousin, who is a nurse, her husband, & his mother. After dinner we played Parcheesi then listened to the Rose Bowl game at 4:45. Some neighbors came in & they all had a field day kidding me as the Ill. score got higher & higher. We had a lot of fun. Sure thought about Dad & Larry. I didn't get to hear the half time stunts at all as Mr. Tittel listened to the East-West game then. I'd sure love to hear about it from Dad or Larry. Did any of you go to the Rose Parade?

It was hard to imagine them having parades or games anyplace, as it snowed here all day yesterday. I was so glad. It really got quite deep in the Bronx. It was a dry snow. I wanted to stay out & play in it, but people think I'm crazy enough when I get so happy to see it snow. As the weatherman says, we're having a "freezing drizzle" today with highest temp. in the low thirties. It doesn't seem too cold though. I slept with my window wide open & didn't even have to put on an extra blanket.

Whoever said people in the Big City were cold & unfriendly just didn't have the right attitude. They're just like anyone from anywhere only more of them.

---

12 The unemployment rate in the U.S. in 1947 was about 8%.

Sure hope Dad if feeling O.K. again. Golly, keep well at "310" as I'd just die if anything happened to any of you while I was away[13].

I enjoyed Mom's letter so much. Yes, Mom, I've been sleeping well. I think that at last I've gotten so that traveling excitement doesn't keep me awake.

Must be up & doing so better close for now.

Bye for now,

Love,

Jean

P.S. Haven't decided what my name will be in Tokyo. Guess I'll see what the Japs can handle best. The assistant mgr. here at K.H. always calls me Norma Jean as he's seen it on my mail & says he likes it.

Jan. 3, 1947

Dearest Folks,

Just a line tonight to let you know the latest with me. I had my final shot this morning—diphtheria. As usual, I'm feeling fine & dandy tonight.

I had an interesting time at the Dispensary though. A man & little boy were ahead of me waiting for shots too. We got to talking & he said he was leaving for Tokyo tonight. He said he was a newspaperman and will be working in G.H.Q. in the Economic Education Division. He wants me to look him & his family up there & they will show me around. He said he's lived there before the war & likes it very much. Gee, it sure made me feel good. He was so interesting as he has been in Egypt & India & has just gotten back from Europe. I have his name & address & can look him up. We said goodbye & "see you in Tokyo." He's leaving at Penn Station tonight & will go to an airfield in Calif. from where they'll be flown to Japan.

Kathryn Cullmer just left. She was over for dinner with me at K.H. Golly she's nice. She always insists in paying for the meals &

---

13 Her parent's home address.

then she gave me two books for a going away gift. They are "From The Top of The Stairs" by Gretchen Finletter & "Green Grass of Wyoming" by Mary O'Hara (who also wrote "My Friend Flicka"). I thought it was lovely of her. I'm planning on sending her something nice from Japan.

Tomorrow, I'll go to Phila. Got such a nice note from Ruth this week. I'm rather dreading it as I hate goodbyes, but that's life.

Got Larry's swell letter today, too, & enjoyed it so much.

Must close for now. Will write in my diary then go to bed. 'Bye now.

All my love,
Norma Jean

Jan. 6, 1947

Darling Mom, Dad, Esther, Larry & Aunt Kate,

Received your wonderful letter just as I was leaving for the War Dept., Mom. It was a masterpiece.

Have lots to tell you—only wish we had more time to explain every little thing. Anyhoo, this is what they told me this morning. I'm sailing from New York Fri., Jan. 10th aboard the Pres. Pope. We will go via Panama Canal & Hawaii, so it will take us 52 days to reach Japan. Boy, the ocean had better agree with me. That means I'll not get to see anyone on the Pacific Coast. I was a little disappointed at first, but in my pep talk to myself decided it was good as I'll get to see so many more things this way—me for the sights. It's balled my packing plans all up though as now I won't have to take train clothes. What a life. Tomorrow, I go to the Port where they will tell me ship details. I'm to have my trunk all ready tomorrow. Six civilians are going with me that I know of—four girls (including me) & two men. They gave us our sealed orders, which we have to carry with us. Am going to enclose my inoculation record. Please keep it in a very safe place. I'll carry one copy with me & they said to keep the other in a different & safe place as it is our only record.

Am expecting Ruth Troy any minute. I got her a room right across the hall from me, so she'll stay all night. It will sure be good to have her with me. We are meeting Kathryn Cullmer tonight for dinner.

Had another wonderful weekend in Phila. Spent more time with Uncle Albert & Aunt Carrie & either saw or talked to others.

The biggest coincidence of my life happened on the train home from Phil. to New York. I got a seat to myself then an Oriental girl came & sat next to me. We didn't say anything for quite a ways then, when we started a conversation, were swept off our feet to find we both came from dear old Compton. Her name is Cathleen Shimomura. She lived at the farm on Central & El Segundo. She was in Edna Royelle's class. She knew Mar Huttinger too as they rode to work together says she. We knew a lot of the same kids & had a field day talking. She was sure surprised at my going to Japan. She said some of the Japanese kids from Compton have a little paper & she's going to put about our meeting in it. She wanted us to have lunch or dinner together, but I didn't know when I could make it. She's going to phone me tonight. She said she knows where I live as she went to CJC & knew where Edna lives. Small world, eh?

Must close now & pack & re-pack. Don't worry about me as I'm armed with plenty of money, maps, clothes, and diaries. I can't believe all this is happening yet but guess I will when I hit the waves. Oh, yes, Uncle Albert fixed me up with sea sickness medicine.

All my love,
Norma Jean

P.S. Forgot one of the main things. My address will be:
Norma Jean Cone, Civilian Employee
A.P.O. 500
c/o P.M.
San Francisco, California
P.S.#2 Couldn't get my address stenciled on my trunk so old Cone has turned artist with a paint brush & white paint.

Jan. 8, 1947

Dearest Folks,

This may reach you after I'm gone but just have to let you know of the last week's details.

Ruth Troy stayed all night with me Monday night. She had a room right across from me here at K.H. She came about 4 Monday; then Kathryn Cullmer came about 5:30, & we all had dinner together. After dinner, I had to come right back to my room as I had to paint my name & address on my trunk. I had madly tried to find somebody to stencil it for me, but no luck. I had to let it go to this late date as they wouldn't give me the address before. Kathryn & Ruth said they'd give moral support. Little did we know what a job we were getting into. The address (4 lines) had to be put on in three places. We measured, drew lines, measured & drew more lines. They both got so excited. Kathryn kept saying "Hell, I bet the damn paint won't stick." She even called Dick to get his opinion. I thought it was all a riot. With both of them breathing down my neck, I began to paint. I painted & painted & drew lines & more lines. Kathryn was here 'til about 11:00 then went back to Brooklyn. Ruth gave up the ship about 12:00 & went to bed while I painted on for about another 1½ hours. I still hadn't finished so got up at 6:30 for the finishing touches. Ruth got up later & we had breakfast together. She went with me to keep an appointment at the Port of Embarkation. After having my fingerprints taken, signing papers, & having passport pictures taken, I went down to Pier number two. I told the man there the quantity of my luggage & where to pick it up. Just as I was leaving he said "Don't bother about putting your name or address on your trunk, as we'll take care of it for you." I couldn't help but laugh. When I met Ruth & told her we both practically had hysterics.

While at the Port of Embarkation, I met some of the people I'll be going with & they seem very nice. There are 63 civilian employees going. It is the General Pope & not President Pope, as I said before. Taking 52 days to get there means we'll be making a lot of stops says Ruth. My pay started January 7, which means I'll have two months salary before I get there.

Ruth & I sure had fun together. We giggled & giggled. I was so tired & she was so excited. We came home, & I finished packing the trunk. Every time we looked at the white lettering we had to laugh. Another thing that was so funny was I almost sat in the paint. Ruth pulled it away in the nick of time. She said she'd look out for my end after that. Later she saved her hat from a crushing fate by looking out for my end. This & other silly things went on constantly until finally I just set a pile of Kleenex between us, so we could laugh in comfort.

She was sure a help in telling me what I'd need to take. She went to the cleaners for me, & she gave me a pair of nylons for a going-away gift. She saw my pictures & decided she'd have to have one of each pose. Kathryn also wanted one. They insisted on paying for them so ordered them yesterday. Ruth had two extra made & is going to send one to each of my grandmothers when they're finished, as I had said I wished I had done it. Isn't she an angel? The ones to gandmas will be with my hair down.

Just came back from dinner with Evelyn & got your special delivery letter, Esther. It's swell. Your outfit sounds sharp.

Had lunch today with that Japanese girl from Compton that I met on the train—Cathleen Shimomura. It seemed so good to talk local stuff with somebody. She's retail statistician at Bloomingdales' store. She took me to lunch at Shrafts.

I thought I'd need more slacks than I had planned for such a long boat ride. I got a three-piece suit at Saks 34th today. It's black, Rayon gabardine, short sleeves, & western design. It has the blouse, slacks, & skirt to match. It fits swell—even long enough. The funniest thing happened; I was in Macy's crowded main floor when a strange man came up to me & said, "When are you sailing?" I asked how he knew I was sailing, & he said he'd seen me yesterday at the Port of Embarkation. He's going to Germany Thurs. & thought maybe I was too. We were both doing last minute shopping. I don't think anything could surprise me anymore after all the surprises I've had lately.

Ruth wanted to come see me off Friday, but they told us no one would be permitted at the pier. Kathryn Cullmer is going with me as far as possible & help me with my bags. She's also going to send the small one home for me as Dick can ship it from his shop. She thinks I should have a Bible & is going to send one to me in Tokyo. She's a card.

I feel bad for having to take all your luggage but will try to remember to send you money for some more, Esther. In the suitcase I'll send home I'll enclose an extra trunk key, in case my trunk ever beats me home you can open it, or if I lose others you can send it to me.

Am planning on writing you often on the boat, then mailing the letters whenever possible. I know I couldn't remember all the details at the end of the trip. Also, have put a cover on my diary & am all set for a travel log.

Will you please mail this & other letters to Larry as my time is so limited now, & I want to tell you all just the same anyhow.

Have been so busy that I haven't gotten excited yet. Not until I saw the frenzy some kids had worked themselves into at the Port yesterday did I realize what I'd been missing. Kathryn & Ruth both said they're more excited than I am. Honestly, haven't even missed any sleep yet.

The weather here is grand. Today was beautiful—clear, sunny & just cold enough to make you feel peppy.

Almost forgot the end of my trunk story. A man from the War Department came at 8 o'clock last night & took it away. I don't think he appreciated all my efforts 'cause he didn't say anything about the lettering.

Ruth left yesterday afternoon about 4:15. She also gave me some throat pills in case of a sore throat. I asked about what other medicine I should take & as per her advice got some aspirin & cascara tablets today. I'm ready for anything now.

Well my darlings, it's time to close for now. Will drop you another line if possible before sailing. Am really looking forward to the trip as I'll see so many things & places. I'd give anything to have you all with me. We'd laugh all across the Pacific I bet. Above all, don't worry about me, because I'll be all right & be having a good time. Just keep well at '310' & I'll do the same.

'Bye for now & oceans of love,
Norma Jean

Jan 10, 1947

Dearest Mom, Dad, Esther, & Aunt Kate,

Here it is—the sailing day has really come. I have everything under control. My bags are packed & I'm waiting for ten o'clock to come as that's when Kathryn will be here.

Didn't we have a nice talk on the phone? I felt so good after we had finished. You all sounded so clear. There was no delay at all. I've had more trouble getting people right here in New York. You all sounded so happy. I hadn't planned on reversing the overtime charges but was running out of quarters. How much more did it cost? It cost me $2.50 for the first three minutes. I was surprised as I thought it would be $5 or $6.

I must tell you about the funny thing that happened to me yesterday. I decided to eat my breakfast in the fountain at the George Washington Hotel next door. Word has gotten around here at Kenwood Hall that I'm going to Japan, & I'm constantly being asked questions. That's why I thought it would be nice to eat in more peaceful surroundings.

For some dumb reason the fountain boy recognized me & insisted on talking. He was eager to make a date with me, & I told him I was going away. He said where, & I nonchalantly said "Japan." He got so excited & started yelling to all the other clerks telling them. Before I got out of there, they fed me about 75¢ worth of breakfast & gave me a check for only a quarter. As I went toward the door all the clerks & some of the customers next to me shouted "Bon Voyage." That's how my peaceful breakfast ended.

I just looked out the window & my weather eye told me it's clear & cold. I'm glad it's cold, as I'd been planning on wearing lots of clothes, which will mean less to pack.

After I finished talking to you last night I washed my hair & went to bed. I really slept very well too. I don't know why but I never have gotten too excited yet.

When Kathryn comes we'll take a taxi to South Ferry where we'll get the Staten Island ferryboat. It's about a half-hour ferry ride.

Must close for now as ten o'clock is getting here fast. Will be thinking of each of you as we "shove off." Have all my gear together &

squared away—guess I can talk right back to the sailors, eh. Be good & keep well.

So long for now.

All my love,
Norma Jean

Two

Dearest Folks:

It is 5:45 & I'm aboard the General Pope. Just hope they'll mail this for us.

The ship is really large. They say there are 2,000 troops, but we never see them. There are also lots of wives & kids.

I was lucky in getting one of the best staterooms. It's large. There are 10 girls in it. The other girls are very nice & I've already got some bloody buddies.

I'm surely thrilled as everything is so perfect. We just finished dinner. Had beef goulash, salad, potatoes, turnips, bread, butter, jam, cakes, coffee & oranges.

Am wearing my blue suit & white blouse but we're all planning on wearing slacks from tomorrow on.

There are a lot of Red Cross girls on the ship too. Also some WACS.[14] We eat in the main dining room with the Captain & officers.

Must close as I'm afraid I'll miss the mail.

> Love to all,
> Norma Jean

---

14 Women's Army Corps.

Jan. 14, 1947
USS General John Pope

Dearest Folks,

This is our fourth day at sea. It's really out of this world. We sailed from New York at 9 p.m. Jan. 10th.

The first day out, an awful lot of people got sick, but I felt swell all the time—haven't missed a meal. For the first two days, the air was a little chilly, but today we're getting the warm tropic breezes.

Am I ever getting spoiled. This is a typical day. Get up in time for 7:30 breakfast. We eat in the officer's mess & have wonderful steward service. Then we go out on the sun deck or promenade deck & sit in deck chairs. Lunch is at 11:30. After this we usually take a long nap.

We get up & go out on the deck & then dress for dinner—4:30. After this, we always watch the gorgeous sunsets, then spend the rest of the evening on the top deck watching the moon & stars come out. What a life, eh?

Sunday, I attended the Protestant church services. It was led by the Army Chaplain. It was very good & we sang lots of good old hymns. Nearly everyone goes—even the troops.

Sunday evening, we had a motion picture "Tangiers." Last night (Monday) we had a dance put on by the Captain. The orchestra isn't too sharp yet. The room was so hot that we left early & went to our favorite spot—topside.

Tonight, we are to have a songfest in the Officer's Lounge.

Yesterday, we had our first fire & life-saving drill. We just all lined up on the starboard side with our life preservers on.

We are now in the Caribbean. We have seen at a distance San Salvador, Haiti, & Jamaica. The Captain announces over the loudspeaker system what we are to pass & where to look. I always get such a thrill out of passing other ships at night & watching them signal each other.

This is really a wonderful ship. It is, or is to be, the flagship for the Army. It is so smooth sailing that unless it's really rough you feel as though you're standing still.

There are 2500 troops below decks, but we don't see much of them. We are classed as first-class passengers along with some Red Cross girls, dependants (wives & children), & Army officers.

I must tell you about my bloody buddies. They are both War Department civilian employees too. One is Marie—a swell girl from Boston, Mass. The other is Louis—a fellow from New York. We three are inseparable. We eat at the same table & take in all the scenery together. It's a riot, because everyone thinks Marie & I are sisters as we do resemble each other, & no one can see where Louis fits in. Of course, we branch out at dances, etc., but "We Three" always bring our friends together for we tell them they're not going to break up our beautiful friendship.

Golly, it's really terrific. We sit on the open top deck, warm breezes, calm & beautiful ocean, beautiful weather, & music from the loudspeaker system.

Am getting a super tan, too. We're all being careful though, as this tropic sun is really penetrating.

Today the PX opened. We can get everything—even soap. There is no tax on anything either.

The meals are swell; we really have a good chef. We never can eat half as much as they give us. You can see some typical menus in the ship paper I'll send.

We're supposed to get to Panama tomorrow. We were talking to the Captain this morning, & he said he didn't think we could get off. "We Three" are hoping he'll change his mind, as Louis has been there & wants to show us around. He also wants to take colored pictures, which he'll share with us. We're just keeping our fingers crossed.

Must close for now, as it's almost time for "chow."

Jan 16

Here we are at Panama. I went to bed at 9:30 then got up at 3 am, as that's when we started going thru the lock. It's very pretty scenery & so interesting. Just as we got to the Canal last night a G.I jumped overboard on a bet. He was an excellent swimmer, but the boat had to go clear around, lower a lifeboat & save him. More fun. Must close & see more scenery.

Love, Norma Jean

1-17-47

Dearest Folks,

Have been at Panama two days & have seen all the sights. Really having super time. It's awfully hot. We all went shopping for summer clothes. I got two dresses, a blouse & white sandals. Don't know when we'll sail on but we're having fun right here. Am waiting for our dates now—Marie, Lou & I.

Love, Norma Jean

January 20, 1947

Dearest Folks,

We left Panama yesterday & we are once more sailing. It's unbelievable to me that the ocean can be so calm. We're in the Pacific now. We forget we're sailing most of the time as the ship is so smooth. It's just like a lake. We're all just trying to keep cool. Boy, is it ever hot.

We were in Panama three days. We all went mad to buy some cool clothes. We docked at Balboa & went to Panama City. I bought a white dress with figures of crocodiles & palm trees, which were predominantly green. It's shantung material I believe. I bought it in a little shop in Panama City for $12.50. At the Commissary we really got bargains. I got a darling blue & white check gingham dress for $4.25. I also got a red checked shirt ($2.25) & a cute pair of flat white sandals

($3.75) at the Commissary. Saturday, buses (USO) were waiting for us in the afternoon & we were taken on a guided tour all over Panama. It lasted about three hours. It was swell. I had my picture taken quite a bit by other kids & will get some from them for you. Every evening we did the town. Most of the places are corny, but there were a few very nice spots. The evenings are wonderful there--just warm enough to feel good wearing a cool dress. Oh, yes, while we were on the tour we had a tropical rain. It just poured for about 5 minutes then stopped suddenly. We also had to wait for a funeral to go by. It was made up of several taxis. The guide said they have to bury them (people not taxis) within 24 hours because of no embalmers. It was a native who died. Sure interesting.

We sailed yesterday at 10:30. After we had gotten about 2 hours out they announced we were returning as the Chief Boatswains Mate had a badly broken arm. We went back to the harbor where a police boat was waiting. The injured man was lowered into it in one of our lifeboats & we once again headed for sea.

The Captain announced this morning that we could see Costa Rica from the starboard side, which would be the last part of Continental North America that we'll see.

The ocean here is infested with sharks & porpoises. You can see them from the decks.

Must hit the deck again before I completely melt in this lounge.

January 23

Hello again,

The weather is not quite as hot as it was & we're getting a little of our ambition back.

I have a slight cold & have been taking cough syrup & pills all day.

We set our watches back for the second time today. We're all famished by the time breakfast rolls around.

I meant to tell you what happened to that G.I. who jumped overboard. He was a Hawaiian & an excellent swimmer. He was court-martialed by the ship's officers & is now in the brig below. The scuttlebutt is that he'll be locked up for 10 years as it counts as desertion & endangering other's lives. I never thought this big ship could turn around so fast & in such a small area.

I don't know exactly where we are today, but yesterday morning we were 400 miles off Acapulco, Mexico. They say we should arrive in Hawaii around next Wednesday or Thursday.

Jan. 29, 1947

Dearest Folks,

We are scheduled to arrive at Honolulu tomorrow so thought I'd add another line. It is raining this morning, but the weather is warm. We are supposed to start seeing some land—Hawaiian Islands this afternoon around four o'clock. We're all eager to land & see Honolulu.

We've been having a good time aboard ship although our imaginations are wearing out trying to think up things to do. Last Saturday, we watched a boxing contest between G.I.'s. The Captain was the referee. All us women were invited to watch from the bridge, so we had super seats. It was fun.

In the evening, we saw the variety show "Rumors Are Flying" put on by the local talent. It was real funny & very good. We are to have another show in two weeks. After the show, we had a dance. It was a little difficult to look graceful dancing as the ship was rolling like a top. More Fun!

Sunday, we all went to church again. Aside from these things nothing has been happening. We have seen a lot of flying fish lately from the decks.

We don't know how long we'll be in Hawaii. According to scuttlebutt it will be from 36 hours to a week. I think it'll be 3 or 4 days probably. It gives you a funny feeling to go ashore after so many days at sea. You feel like the ship is still rolling, & we all go staggering down the street.

At Panama, we left all the dependants, so we've had no wives or children with us since. We hear we're to pick up a lot more at Hawaii though. The waiters can hardly wait—a lot of babies between 6 months & two years will join us.

I don't think we'll go to Manila, but nothing is certain. That is where all the troops are going, & they'll probably leave us off at Yokahama first.

Must close for now. Sure hope you're all well. Aloha!

Love,
Norma Jean

P.S. We've been given Japanese language books & have been having fun trying it out—looks impossible.

Jan. 31, 1947

Hello again,

A line before going ashore. We docked this morning at Honolulu. It was beautiful coming into the islands last night. I've never seen such a gorgeous sunset in all my life. It was setting just as we passed the volcano, Mauna Loa. It was a wonderful sunny morning, & Honolulu is so pretty. An Army band was there to meet us as usual & of course played Aloha Oe. Lou is taking me ashore, & we plan to see everything. He really has the old sight-seeing spirit. Everybody's getting leis & wearing them around their necks.

Must close & go again.

All my love,
Norma Jean

P.S. Please send this to Larry as I'm running out of time.

Jan. 31, 1947

Dear Esther:

Am at the Honolulu P.O., so just had to drop you a line from here. Just mailed some packages home—hope they get there okay. I'm mad about Honolulu—really beautiful. We went to Waikiki yesterday. We have to be at the ship at 12 o'clock & the rumor is we'll sail today, but we're hoping for more time here.

Aloha, N.J.

February 1, 1947

Dearest Family,

Here we are once more at sea & our visit at Hawaii seems like a dream. We all wanted to stay longer but no such luck.

We got shore passes at Noon, day before yesterday, which were good until Noon yesterday. We docked at 9:30 in the morning. Coming into these islands was wonderful. It was a bright & beautiful morning. The islands are so green & have such beautiful hills & then palm trees along the shore. As usual an Army band met us at the dock. When we got off we went to Honolulu City, which is just a short way from the pier. We saw the sights there, then went to Waikiki beach. It is nice but has too much coral for good swimming they say. The breakers break way out—how I'd love to have our wind bag here. We didn't go in, as we thought we could later, so didn't bring our suits. The Royal Hawaiian Hotel is located right at Waikiki beach—it doesn't look too exclusive from the outside. We ate dinner at a real cute restaurant at Waikiki called the Beachwalk. In the evening, we went dancing & saw some nightlife. It's more fun as you always are seeing some other couples from your ship everywhere you go, & we're practically one big happy family now. We all managed to drop in for a hamburger before the night was over—the first since we left the U.S., & boy did they ever taste good. Yesterday morning, Marie & I went into town & did some shopping. I mailed packages to Larry, Mom, Dad, & Esther. If any of you don't get them, let me know as they were all insured, & I have the receipts. Just hope every thing is okay as I did such a fast job. I bought myself a flashy Hawaiian print shirt & a pair of Gold Cross black shoes. We went back to the ship in the afternoon for lunch as our passes were up.

After lunch, a group of Hawaiian women were on the pier to entertain us. They sang songs & danced (the hula of course). They wore leis & grass skirts. It was sure good. The G.I.'s practically fell off the rails. The funniest thing was when the solo hula dancer came over to our pal (a Warrant Officer) & insisted he dance with her. He was a good sport & was shown the fundamentals of the hula before a vast audience. Lou, who is a camera bug, got some good shots of it & we're dying to see them. What a riot. They told us our passes were extended, so we dashed back to town for a final look. The Warrant Officer went with us, & with all the fun, we felt we were with a celebrity for sure. We came back at 4 o'clock & we sailed at 5:30. The Army Band was playing sad songs, G.I.'s were shooting firecrackers & throwing confetti, & everyone felt sad to have to leave so soon. The band played Aloha Oe as we pulled away from the pier & everyone threw their leis overboard, for that is good luck. The sun was setting & was gorgeous—a huge orange ball. It got dark fast, & we saw the lights of the harbor & the city fading from sight.

February 8, 1947

Hello again,

We're just getting out of a storm at sea. It's lasted about five days. Not many have gotten sick & it's been rather fun & exciting. Most of the dishes & all of the glasses in the mess hall broke, so one night we just had cold cuts until they could get into their reserves. The first days the boat pitched from bow to stern & the last few it's been rolling from side to side. Lou took a picture of a wave breaking over the bow. We were on the bridge & had to duck from the spray way up there. There have been a few casualties from falling or being thrown. Last night a G.I. broke his leg. I never thought I could sleep & be thrown around so much, but I sure can. The paper said we had forty-foot waves so you can imagine. It's very windy, but the air is not too cool. We have more fun at the dinner table trying to keep our chairs from sliding away from the table & our plates out of our laps.

We crossed the International Date Line. The Captain announced we would go to bed Monday night & wake up Wednesday morning, so we just lost a day.

I guess we're not going to Manila. They keep changing their minds (rather Washington changes it for them), but we're on the course to Yokohama according to the marked maps on the wall. All the troops aboard are to be stationed in the Philippines.

We've been knocking ourselves out thinking up things to do. Marie & Lou were both kind of sea sick so that limited us. We'd just get started at a game & they'd make a dash for the nearest hatchway. We've played everything—usually its rummy or (of all things) Chinese Checkers. Yesterday another girl & I got so tired of sitting we went on the top sides & ran around the stack & jumped rope. Everyone's back to grammar school games.

Tonight, we're to have another variety show & dance. I don't think there will be much dancing at this rate of rolling though. Oops—we've just had another big jolt so if you're having trouble reading this you'll know why. They say the jolts come from the rudder lifting out of the water then hitting a wave head on.

We got a new head steward at Hawaii. The man's mad for food. Gad we've never seen such meals. I'll get some menus if I can. I thought the food before was out of this world, but this stops me. They keep wanting to give you seconds, too. The bread is baked fresh daily. The strawberry ice cream has real big berries all through it—think I'll marry the chief cook of the General John Pope.

We had another fire & abandon ship drill yesterday. We just all put our life preservers on & go to the promenade deck at the sound of the signal.

Three

Dear Mom, Dad, Esther, Larry & Aunt Kate,

I'm in but can't believe it. We docked yesterday afternoon. We're living in temporary housing units until we find out where we'll work. Golly, we feel so strange & confused. It's really more Americanized than I thought it would be. The Japanese people look pretty ragged & cold to me. I can see where I'm going to be spoiled fast here. We get wonderful table service where we eat. In the morning you just get dressed, as the maid makes your bed, cleans your room, & washes anything you want washed.

I went to the Post Office this morning, but there was no mail. Guess it just hasn't caught up with us yet. It's a funny feeling not to have heard from home for so long.

Marie went directly to Tokyo, so "We Three" were separated. My pal Lou is here. We saw the town together last night. He's been so nice to me. He spent four years in Trinidad & really knows how to get around & how to get along with the locals.

The weather is cold but clear & sunny. My New York winter clothes feel darn good. It feels so wonderful to wear dresses again as I wore practically nothing but slacks aboard ship.

Must close for now as it's time to go for my personnel appointment. I'll find out what's cooking, then write again. I have plenty of money left from the trip & a month's pay coming up.

More real soon.

All my love,
Norma Jean

P.S. Don't write 'til I tell you my new address. I should get it tomorrow.

Have been madly cramming from the Japanese language book we were given aboard ship.

> *The trip from New York to Japan took less than the 52 days planned, because the ship did not go via the Philippines as was usual. In her first letter home, Norma Jean mentions how ragged and cold the Japanese people appeared to be. This is one of the few references to how desperately poor the people were when Japan surrendered. Also, there is no mention at this point of how much hunger existed in occupied Japan. General McArthur had, in fact, ordered the American troops not to eat any Japanese food, because the Japanese needed it so badly. Many city dwellers were trading their personal possessions to rural people for food. From the letters, it is clear that the American occupiers were well cared for by the Japanese, and fared quite well.*
>
> *On arrival in Japan, Norma Jean made her first transpacific telephone call. This was a significant expense in 1947. The $12 charge for three minutes was at least $120.00 in 21st Century dollars.*

Feb 17, 1947

Dearest Folks,

Have been meaning to write you everyday but expected to get my address before this. So much has happened since I talked to you. It was sure good to hear your voices & to know that everything at 310 is under control. I still haven't gotten any mail.

We had some real excitement the afternoon after I called you. At 4:15 the Quonset hut right next to mine burned down. Twenty-three girls lost everything they had. Most were girls who came on the same ship as I did. It was a terrible loss, but no one was hurt. We felt especially sorry for one girl, as she phoned home the day before & found that her mother had died the day we docked. She was practically hysterical when she found all her things were burned up. We were all moved to new quarters that night. They were not quite finished—that's why temporary housing in Quonset huts.

Saturday, I moved to Tokyo. Am living in the Old Kaijo Hotel. It's very large & nice.

My roommate is Emilie Graf (the Japanese all call her Emory). She's from San Jose, Calif. & very nice. She's about my age & went to Univ. of Wash.

We have our own maid here who does our cleaning, washing, & ironing daily. We're on the fourth floor & the dining room is on the third. Japanese girls wait on you hand & foot. You just raise your cup & they come running with more coffee. The food is good. We have nice linen tablecloths & napkins & pretty china to eat on. Gad am I getting spoiled.

Marie is at the Park Hotel here & we get together quite a bit. Lou came with me to Tokyo but is assigned to work in Yokohama.

I went to work today for the first time. I don't know for sure how it will be, but I'm thinking good. Our hours are 8:30-11:30 & 1:30 to 4:30. I'm the only white girl so far as it's just new. I work in an office with a Colonel, two Majors, & two Privates. We just talked most of today. They took me to the Officer's Mess at noon. They call for me &

bring me home in a Jeep, so I don't have to walk at all. I'm in the same office as was that Colonel who stole the diamonds, so it's real exciting.[15] A Lieutenant was telling me today that there are 1700 Japanese working at the Bank now. It formerly was the Japanese Reserve Bank. It's so big you could easily get lost.

It started snowing here the afternoon after I called you. It's been very cold, but the sun shines during the day most of the time.

So far, I haven't missed a day writing in my diary. Have had more fun with the horoscopes in the front of it. On the ship, kids kept asking me to read their horoscopes to them.

---

15 This is discussed in more detail in subsequent letters.

Wednesday, Feb. 19

Hi:

Just got my address yesterday so will at last mail this. Am on my way to work so must dash. To be continued later.

New address:

Norma Jean Cone, Civilian Employee

Tokyo-Kanagawa Military Gov't. District

APO 181

C/O P.M.

San Francisco, Calif.

Please send this to Larry as I haven't written to him yet.

P.S. How did they let you know I was going to call?

Feb. 23, 1947

Dearest Folks,

It's Sunday morning here in Tokyo & the weather is clear, cold & sunny. I just got back from church services with my roommate & a Captain. Am scheduled for a tea dance & buffet supper starting at two this afternoon so will write between times. Just finished dinner—soup, chicken, escalloped potatoes, lettuce, vegetables, cocoa & chilled fruit cocktail.

Still haven't gotten a bit of mail—it just takes time I guess.

I unpacked my trunk the other day & found everything shipped perfectly. My radio plays swell. We can only get two stations—a Jap one & an American one. We have all the best programs without any advertising. We hear stateside programs direct from Los Angeles quite often—especially news.

We were a little early for church this morning, so Emilie & the Capt. took me on a tour of Tokyo. It must have been a beautiful spot before the war, as the buildings that are still standing are beautiful. The streets are very wide with lots of parkways.[16]

Yesterday, I saw a demonstration for the first time. In the street below my window a lot of Japanese marched & carried banners & were led by bands. We don't know what it was all about since we can't read their signs anyhow. They marched on into the Palace grounds.

> *The march probably was in response to the Yoshida cabinet elected at the first general election under the new U.S.-style constitution. This new constitution gave women the right to vote, guaranteed basic freedoms and civil liberties, abolished nobility, and made the emperor the "spiritual ruler" of Japan, taking away virtually all his political powers. Elections were held in April 1947 for national and local offices.*

The place where the tea dance is to be held is very interesting. It is now an Officer's Club, but before the war belonged to a Japanese Duke. The house & grounds are beautiful. The house is low & sprawling with big marble fireplaces.

Work is still good as far as I'm concerned. Starting this week we won't work any Saturdays, which means I can get in some good tours as many last over Saturday & Sunday. There isn't much to my job, but it's a very interesting spot to be. They're taking an inventory of all the stuff in the bank for the first time & they find the most interesting things—like piles of diamonds & gold. I'm still the only American woman there. It's really a riot. The Col. & I lead the parade of Majors & Capts. when we go & come from lunch. Am getting a big kick out of it all. They all take things so seriously when the Col. is around.

> *According to the military newspaper "Stars & Stripes," in testimony at Colonel Edward Murray's trial, "…the priceless collection of 250,000 carats of precious gems in the Bank of Japan vaults was*

---

16 About one-half of the urban housing was destroyed by American bombing, and the Tokyo population had shrunk by more than one-half.

> *in a 'confused condition' with diamonds mixed indiscriminately with 'worthless debris'."*
> *Also, in testimony at Colonel Murray's trial, Tokuo Suzuki said he took 106,000 carats of diamonds in Thermos bottles from vaults of Mitsui Trust Co. to the Bank of Japan on October 18, 1945. That horde was estimated to be worth more than $50 million dollars.*

Have been to the Ernie Pyle Theatre several times.[17] It's really nice & strictly for Americans. The stage is immense & has revolving stages. They always have a show & a stage show. Last night I saw "Abie's Irish Rose." The stage show "Showtime" was very good. Someone said an article & pictures about it would be in some stateside magazines so be sure & take notice if it is.

I should be able to save money here as there's nothing to spend it on. All trains & buses are free, meals are only a quarter, & my entertainment is free. Things at the PX are cheaper too & no taxes. Am not going to do much souvenir buying for a while, although it's sure a temptation. Am going to look everything over first. Also, the money & inflated prices are something it takes time to learn about. We don't use any American money. It's all G.I. scrip or yen. The legal exchange is now fifteen yen to one dollar.

Am going to be needing more shoes, I can see right now. I ruined two pair on the ship, & the rough streets here are murder on shoes. Soo—if you see any sharpies how about sending them? Either heels or flats will do. Guess you'd better not send anything until I start getting mail here. Just to be sure my address is okay—these darn P.O.'s!

Have sure been thinking about you & hope "oils well". Must close & dress for the big date. Bye now

All my love,
Norma Jean

---

17 The rechristened name of the Takarasuo Gekiho.

Feb. 26, 1947

Dearest Folks,

It's a rainy night & we're listening to "Duffy's Tavern" & I'm trying to catch up with a few letters. Still haven't gotten any mail but now I've got the courier at the office asking at the P.O. for me.

We had quite a little earthquake this morning. It's the second one I've felt so far. Neither has scared me. Most of the buildings are earthquake proof so I feel pretty safe.

Have been as busy as usual. We were going to the Ernie Pyle Theatre's first year's anniversary. We went early, but the seats were all sold out. I haven't seen such a crowd since the last time I went to Macy's. You could hardly squeeze into the lobby. They had two stage shows, "Blue Skies," & a speech by some general. We went again last night & saw the show & one stage show—very good.

My Sunday date turned out very good. At the tea dance they had a large orchestra, & there weren't many people—just super for dancing. The buffet supper was swell—lots of good food. A four-piece string ensemble played dinner music for this. In the evening, another orchestra played for dancing & some Japanese put on a floorshow. Sure seems funny to watch them do Spanish rumbas.

Work goes on as usual. Golly, I've never done so little & gotten so much. Am still the only gal in the office—the boys are all very nice to me & make me feel right at home.

Saturday, some kids from Yokohama that came on the Pope with me are coming to see me & Tokyo. As we say, a "Dopes from the Pope" party.

Must close for tonight, sweetie-pies. As we say about so many things—this was a sco-shee (short) note. We'll keep the courier hot on the trail for my mail, as I can hardly wait to get the good word from youse guys. My maid was just in & briefed on some more Japanese. I just learned sa-re-yo-na-la (the way it sounds) (good-bye). So that really stops me.

All my love,
Norma Jean (in Japanese, it's Jean-son)

Four

March 3, 1947

Dearest Folks,

Am home on my two-hour lunch period so will drop a line to you.

I feel so happy, because I just received some mail. The G.I. mail courier comes in beaming today & dashes over with my mail. I received Mom's & Dad's letters, which were mailed on Feb. 10th & Larry's mailed on February fourth. Was so sorry to hear of Esther's illness & sure hope you're feeling tops again, kiddo.

I had a swell time this weekend. Friday night, I went to an Officer's Club in the country. Emilie & I double dated. Saturday, we had a riot at the "Dopes from the Pope" party. Sunday morning, six of us D. from the P. went on a Red Cross Tour to Kamakura. The biggest & best Buddha in all of Asia is said to be the one there. It rained like mad all day, but we had fun anyway. We got into rural Japan & saw (& smelled) real atmosphere. We went on a train then A.R.C. (American Red Cross) buses, & guides took us on up to the shrines. They served us lunch in a Japanese tearoom. We did a little souvenir shopping (that's where I got this stationery) then we went to Yokohama. I stayed there & had dinner; then Lou brought me into Tokyo, where we saw the show & stage show at the Ernie Pyle.

Guess my mail will get to me all right, so anytime you find some cute shoes, I'd appreciate your sending them. Also, I need a new black purse. I want a small, dressy one. Also, would you stick in a few 10 cent tubes of lipstick I can give my maid for tips. Kleenex is very hard to get so maybe you could pack a few in. It takes around two months for packages to get here regular mail & about two weeks air mail. I'm not in any desperate hurry for anything, however. Will get paid in two weeks & will send some money home then. Better get good shoes, as it's murder on them here.

The band is playing outside which means the changing of the guard & time for me to meet the "Jeepoo".

Love,
Norma Jean

March 12, 1947

Dearest Folks,

Time goes so fast. I just realized how long it had been since I'd last written you. I haven't gotten any more mail at all than the one letter from you & Larry. I keep thinking I'll surely get a stack one of these days. I'm sure wondering how everything at 310 is coming.

We are having beautiful sunny spring days. They are cold but pretty. The trees are just beginning to blossom.

Last Monday, we had to turn in all our Gov't Scrip money as the series number was being changed. We had the afternoon off to take care of this. I took a Red Cross Tour of Tokyo after my business was taken care of. It was a swell tour—we even got to see the Emperor's Throne in the House of Peers at the Diet Bldg. We had a Japanese guide who told about all the buildings & sights.

Today, the open exchange rate was changed from 15 yen to 50 yen to one dollar. They're trying to stop the black market practices—it will take more than this. The black mark't rate is around 100 yen to one dollar & you know the G.I.'s & Americans.

I haven't gotten paid any money yet. It will probably be about two weeks before I do, too. It's a good thing living is cheap or I'd be on the dole. My meals are 25¢. My room is $6 a month & is deducted from my check. Laundry is free, transportation, & telephone are free & dry cleaning is very cheap. The only thing to spend money for is souvenirs.

Silk material is not expensive here. I've bought some for you & will be sending it on later. I'm going to have some dresses made when I find a good seamstress—some are good & some lousy. None of them use patterns—you just show them the picture of the dress you want. If you see a dress which would be appropriate for dances, tea parties, etc. would you please send it to me. I can get along for work with my clothes but this nightlife is rough on the situation. As summers are very hot here, I'd like some cool, dressy dresses. Get good ones & I'll reimburse you when my paycheck comes. There's no rush, but it takes so long for packages sometimes that I want to get things for spring & summer now. The gals here also order clothes from Charm, Vogue, etc. I ordered a blouse this way. The clothes at the PX are very plain & when they get a new shipment in, everyone dashes down, & you see the same thing on women all over town. We are rationed on nylons— one pair a month. They are real nice though & only cost $1.05. Am sure glad for the ones you gave me, Mom.

I didn't go on the trip I was planning last weekend. Our transportation got all screwed up, & we missed the ship at Yokohama. Instead I stayed in Yokohama Saturday night with girl friends, & we had another "Dopes from the Pope" get-together Sunday.

Am planning on going to Mt. Fuji Sunday in a Jeep if all goes well. It's not too far. I can see it from my window plainly on a clear day.

It's so hard to write when I haven't heard from you—just hope these P.O. boys get on the ball. I asked for mail in Honolulu but didn't get any. It's funny as other kids got mail.

Must close for now.

All my love,
Norma Jean

March 18, 1947

Dearest Folks,

I just received two letters & was <u>so</u> glad. One was from Mom, which was mailed Mar. 8, & the other from Larry mailed March 9. A Major brought one for me & a G.I. the other. I have all of them on the trail for my mail now.

I sure did enjoy your newsy letter, Mom. The food here is good, but I sure did drool when I read about the hot apple pie alamode. I see my press agents are still on the job—I'm keeping a scrapbook, & I put my clipping in it.

Life is still wonderful in Tokyo. Saturday night, I went to two formal dances. We stayed for the floorshow at one then went to another—more fun! Sunday, we started out in a Jeep for Mt. Fuji. It was such a bad day though, as it snowed a little in the morning, then rained all day. After about an hour of bumping along we got so cold & stiff, we decided to call it off until a better day. We got to Yokohama just in time for a hot lunch, which really tasted good.

Emilie & I are having a swell time planning our room. We're going to make bedspreads, chair covers, etc. We've signed up to rent a sewing machine at the PX. We're really a pair. Every night, we have a brainstorm. We've decided to go to class to learn Russian together. Our maid teaches us Japanese. We'll probably change our minds several times before enrolling. Also, one night we decided to buy Japanese Mandolins & have a duet in Room 424.

I sent a package home last Saturday for father's birthday. I sent some white silk in it. If you want any more of this silk tell me, as it's not expensive. That was $4.15 for six yds. (You have to buy it in six yd pcs.) Also, I sent some snapshots—I have some just like them, so do anything you want with those. I'd like you to send them to Larry, as I didn't send him any.

I bought a camera of my own. It's a Kodak Bantam so can take lots more pictures.

Must close as it's time to go back to the vaults.

All my love,
Norma Jean

March 19, 1947

Dearest Folks,

Received your super letters of Mar. 12 today. As the Col. was sick today, the Capt. told us we could "button up" early, so I will dash off a line before dinner. I enjoyed the clippings you enclosed.

I was glad you asked me questions, cause I forget what I've told you & take so many things for granted about this Japanese living. Will answer the questions from your letters gladly. About the clothes situation—they say summers are really hot here. I would like a couple of dressy, cool dresses from home, as I previously mentioned. Guess you'd better send a few cool cottons for work for me—doesn't have to be new just some of my old ones will be okay. Am still on the look out for a good seamstress, as we pay them with yen, & it costs us very little to have things made. I can get scrumptious silk & Rayon at the PX. I weigh around 135 I think, so better get the clothes plenty roomy for you, Esther. Shoes are really the vital thing. The PX usually doesn't have a single pair, & if they do they're real stupid looking. We can get beautiful lingerie there, though. None of the Japanese stores carry stateside clothes—just kimonos, etc. Yes, we can get permanents here. There is a beauty shop right in our hotel. I went down the other day to find out about a perm. Natch, the Japanese beauticians can't speak a word of English. The sign said Cold Waves Machine, or Machineless perms were all $4.00. The gals here say they're pretty good. We can get a pretty good selection of cosmetics at the PX. They are good brands & a lot cheaper than at home, as there's no tax on anything. Those girls who lost their clothes in the fire are having a rough time. They bought what they could at the PX, the Red Cross gave them a few things, & now they're just waiting for things to be sent them from home. One girl who had previously been a model in New York had $2,000 invested in her wardrobe. All she had when she got here was a wet, smoky sweater. I was with her when she opened her burned trunk—she was really a sad tomato.

I meant to tell you that it would be a good idea to wash or clean everything I send from here pretty good before you use it. I know one gal who got a crazy rash from a bracelet she bought here. The Dr. said it was something the workman had. We've all got to go regularly for booster inoculations. All our food is either shipped in or is grown on a special farm near here. We can't eat any Japanese food. Our water is highly chlorinated & is marked if it is fit to drink or not. I understand our maids have to have frequent physical exams. They seem to be very clean, & the ones here come from the better families they say. The Japanese as a whole seem to be pretty clean. Lots of them wear gauze bandages over their mouths & noses in order to keep from getting colds, etc. Other than the <u>strong</u> fish odor, it's not bad.

I don't think I told you about their driving on the left here. All traffic is on the left hand side of the streets. You're supposed to stay on the left on the sidewalks, stairs, etc. too.

I sure do like Emilie. She's so considerate & is loads of fun. We're going to fix our room real cute then take pictures of it to send you.

My iron broke on the ship—Lou said the current was too strong for it there. He's fixing it for me, but I don't need it here anyway as the maids have one. They iron beautifully & are insulted if you iron anything. They are pretty sensitive. If you sit at one table a few times, they knock themselves out to please you. Then, if you don't sit there, they feel hurt.

The weather here is still cold. Cherry trees are scheduled to blossom about the 10th of April.

I'm having such a wonderful time. I only wish all of you could be here too. It's really <u>much</u> nicer than I expected. Time goes so fast as there's so much going on all the time.

Must close as it's dinnertime—I'm still a chow-hound & wouldn't be late for a meal. Bye now.

Love,
Norma Jean

P.S. Thanks for the picture. When I saw that, I knew you were all still on the ball. Still haven't gotten paid. It will be a small fortune by the time it gets to me.

March 23, 1947

Dearest Mom,

It is so wonderful to be getting letters from you. I got yours of March 14th & the registered one last week. Am so glad you sent back my income tax forms. I'm planning on getting it taken care of tomorrow.

It is Sunday evening, & I'm very tired as Emilie, Ginny, & I went to Atami today. Golly, it was beautiful. It is South of Tokyo & took about two & a half hours by train. It is located on the ocean. We spent the day at Atami Hotel. Huge cliffs overlook the blue ocean. It was a beautiful sunny day & the cherry trees were all in bloom. We all have a slight sunburn as we lay on the beach for quite a while. We took our lunch & had a super picnic. After lunch, we went shopping around the little village, then came home.

We had more fun all week—stupid things kept happening all the time it seemed. For instance, one night the phone in our room rang. I answered & a fellow said "Hello, Jean!" Then another fellow's voice said "Hello Jean." The character at the switchboard had plugged two calls for me in at the same time. I thought it was so funny. I just died laughing. All three of us could hardly talk for giggling. We finally decided one should call a little later.

Yesterday, Emilie & I bought flutes. We expect our neighbors to start pounding our walls anytime. As E. says, we sound more like fish dealers than snake charmers. We have also added two gold fish to our happy household. We now have dwarfed trees, camellia bushes, flowers & fish. The wonderful part is the maids take good care of all of them for us.

I was very surprised & happy about that letter from Bd. of Soc. Work Examiners. Thanks a million for sending in the five dollars for me, as I wanted it just like that. Guess you'd better not send the certificate, as I'm afraid of losing it here.

I will start working on the ham-radio station deal & try to call during Larry's vacation if it's possible.

Yes, the phone call cost only $12.00 for three minutes. If you ever want me to call any special time just let me know. I'll also feel free to give you a ring every so often. We have to make reservations a couple of days in advance for the hour we want.

I still haven't gotten paid, & it's liable to be a week or two yet. It's unbelievable all the things I've done & seen on so little money. They deduct my room rent ($6.00) from our checks. We buy our meal tickets ($23.75) for every month. Our meals are 25¢ each. They deduct nothing for board or meals aboard ship.

About that shirt I sent, Dad. I didn't know what size to get. If it's not right tell me. I paid three dollars for it, but since the yen exchange has changed they are now $1.55 so if you want any more tell me. Also, give me the right shirt sizes for you & Larry.

I like my work a lot. My lucky stars were with me again. Since I was the first gal there I get to do the "fun" jobs. I'm doing mostly bookkeeping & the others have to do straight typing.

The Indians are now on guard duty at the Palace. It's so interesting to watch their parade. They wear colorful uniforms & turbans. I took a picture of them yesterday & hope it turns out good.

Another thing I was going to ask you. Bullocks advertises in some magazines & lots of the girls order things from them. Would it be okay if I used your charge account? It would be a lot simpler for me, as I wouldn't have to bother with figuring mailing, tax, etc. I'd rather just send you money. I understand they have to get your okay, too.

The Japanese sandman is creeping up on me fast so must close. 'Bye for now.

Love,
Norma Jean, R.S.W.

March 26, 1947

Dearest Mom, Dad, Esther, & Aunt Kate,

It is a beautiful sunny Saturday morning & I have the whole day to do just what I want. Think I'll see about taking a little tour & getting some pictures.

How do you like my stamp? I bought it in a Japanese shopping arcade across the street. The characters are Norma Jean in Japanese. I had an awful time with the little man, as he first couldn't say Norma. The stamp is white ivory with a bird on it. It comes in an alligator box, which is lined with red velvet & print material.

I received your wonderful letter & fashion pictures yesterday, Esther. They were both wonderful. Emilie & I poured over the pictures all lunch hour. It only took six days for them to get here, so I feel my mail route is really established now. Am dying to get the packages you mailed. I'm sure the boys will bring them to me as soon as they come. All our mail is delivered to us at work.

Was sorry to hear of Aunt Kate's being unable to find a place to live in Long Beach. It would be so nice if she could live near us permanently. I thought housing would surely be eased up there by this time. Guess you'll have to join me, Aunt Kate, no housing problem here!

About the wristwatch problem, Esther—Mae--we can sign up for them on the critical list & get them at a good price I understand. I don't know if I'd be allowed to send one home, but I'll find out. I'll put my name on the list anyhow, as it takes quite awhile. I'm getting a real good camera, an Argosy, with a light meter this way. It will cost about one-half as much as in the States. It will take me a while to learn how to use it, as they look kind of complicated to me.

Would you like to hear Emilie's & my latest brainstorm? This we're really excited about. They issued a new order yesterday saying that if you stay 'til the end of your contract, they'll arrange the transportation home via Europe if you want. They pay as much of it as it would cost the shortest way from Japan to your home. I'm really going to save my money & go home that way. Emilie is planning on going to school in Switzerland next year & is planning now on meeting me in the spring of '49 & we'll go around Europe together & come home to California together. Doesn't that sound like a dream? She's so wonderful to travel with I'd just love to have it this way. A lot can happen before then but we'll dream about it anyway. Right now, Emilie is kind of serious about a Lieutenant who is General Casey's son, so anything can happen.

The rainy season is on here, & it rains about every other day. They say it will be this way until June. It looks so green & pretty & the sun shines brightly the days it doesn't rain. Must close for now.

P.S. Keep the pictures I'm sending, as I'll have more developed & enlarged. Took them with my little Kodak Bantam.
P.S.#2 Haven't been paid yet but hope to be next week. It's one way of saving money.

Five

Dearest Esther & all,

I received the super package & your swell letter yesterday, Esther.
I just love the darling Easter card. It doesn't even seem like Easter
here. It will be a big weekend though as Army Day is the following
Monday, which means lots of parades. They've been practicing madly
for it.

Everything you sent was so nice, & I appreciate it so much. Am
so glad you included a calendar. We just fixed up a desk & had no
calendar for it, or for our room. The purse is exactly what I wanted.
It's small but long enough to put my comb in. You were so generous
with the lipsticks, & my maids really enjoy them for tips. I had no
Kleenex at all, so you can imagine how welcome that was. Was very
glad you included the program, cards, & lip tissues. You are always
so thoughtful & seem to know just what I'd like. I Scotch taped your
card & the cute ones from Yvonne on our sliding closet door, & they
look real nice.

I had a nice weekend. Saturday morning, I went to the ham
radio station. It's located in the New Kaijo Hotel right around the
corner from me. I gave them your name, address, phone number
& Jimmy's name & call number. When they contact him they will
call me up. They have phone connections & I may talk to you right
from the phone in my room. Their call number is J2AAO. My

phone number is 267251 (they change the phone number quite often, so maybe it would be best to say Room 424 at Old Kaijo Hotel). It's very hard to say when I'll call, as the weather makes a difference. It probably will be a Sat. or Sun. morning for me (Fri. or Sat. evening for you).

After that, I went over to the Palace grounds & watched a General reviewing troops for Army Day dress practice. In the afternoon, I watched a Japanese relay race. It was a beautiful day, & I hated to come in at all. In the evening, I went to a dance at the Cavalry Officers Club. Sunday, Emilie & I went to church. We went to services at the Dai Ichi bldg. (MacArthur's Hdqts) as Emilie works there & just took time off for services. In the afternoon, Ginny & I walked all over the place. We were going out that night but got so sleepy from our fresh air exercises we just couldn't go.

I'm so busy I hardly have time for anything. Emilie & I are in the midst of bedspread making. Last night, we went to our first Russian class & now say our Russian alphabet to each other while sewing. I'm also gathering material on Japanese customs & social life, which I work on in spare moments. If I ever go back to school, it will be wonderful material for a thesis.

I was glad you told me how the package shipped to you arrived. That little dish wasn't very expensive & I'll know to pack things like that better. They have such pretty china here I've been tempted to send some of it. Guess I'd better have a wooden box made for that.

Am very glad you mailed those summer dresses as they'll be perfect for work. One other thing I'll need for this summer is a pair of white gloves. I think some "shorties" would be cute with summer dresses.

I guess Larry will be home when this gets there. Did you color eggs this year? Remember how we colored them last year & sent Larry some? We had more fun. I just remembered you & I were both feeling kind of sick last Easter, Esther. I had eaten that bad potato salad & was not even interested in food at all on Easter Sunday. I bet Margaret Cooney will enjoy Easter this year. Here I go rambling on & on. I'd talk for a week solid right now if I could drop in at 310.

I had the best time at work today. I went down in the vaults & saw millions & millions of dollars worth of stuff. Can't tell you much about it but someday I'll be able to. It's really an experience.

Emilie just came & said she's finished so will join her at dinner. Bye now. Happy Easter to each of you.

All my love,
Norma Jean

April 8, 1947

Dearest Mom, Dad, Esther, & Larry,

What a wonderful mail call I had today! I received the dress, corde' purse & Mom's super letter. I love all of them. I dashed home & tried the dress on, & it fits swell. I hung it up & was going to give the maid special instructions on how to press it. When I came back from lunch, she had already done a beautiful job, & she probably knows more about material than I'll ever know. It will be perfect for this summer. The days are warm now, so it won't be long. The corde' bag is darling—what good taste you have. It will hold lots, too, the way it's made.

I also received real cute Easter cards from Yvonne & Mrs. & Mr. Fanshier. I've got them all lined up on the sliding closet door. I think the one from my family is real cute, & I like the way you all signed it.

I got the tennis shoes at the most appropriate time. The Captain just told us we'd have the afternoon off, so Helen & I decided to put our tennis shoes on & play tennis. She suggested later that we play golf, so that's what we did. Golly, it was fun. We went out to a country club &

took a golf lesson from a professional for only ¥20, which included the use of clubs. We had dinner out there too—luscious steak. It didn't cost anything, as we just gave them our regular meal ticket. We're all set to go again on our next afternoon off.

It certainly didn't seem like Easter to me. The weekend was crowded with parades. I liked the Eighth Army parade Monday best. Gen Eichelberger (on the ground) reviewed it. There were lots of tanks, & there were P80's flying overhead. Friday afternoon, the Japanese had a big election parade. Thousands marched carrying banners & flags of all nations. There were many Russian flags & insignias. The demonstration was by the WFTU.[18] They sang the Marseillaise with an Oriental accent as they marched. Life is so exciting here—never a dull moment.[19]

I spent Sunday in Yokohama. We visited Chinatown there. I was surprised to find so many Russians living there. They are White Russians who were kicked out of Russia in the revolution in 1918. They own little shops & live just like the natives. Most are very blond & large in size.

Emilie & I were invited to a Japanese home last night. Our maid asked us to her house. I'm not sure whether we were supposed to go, so don't tell all the Generals you know about it. She lives in a very typical Japanese home in Tokyo. It's simple, clean, & artistic. We took her little brother some candy & her mother some cigarettes. They gave each of us pretty wall plaques. Her little brother, Toshi, is learning English in school, so he was the chief interpreter. We all sat around with English-Japanese dictionaries & had a nice visit.

I must tell you about the telegram I sent you. They have lists of greetings & you pick out three, which cost 60¢ to send any place. Don't want to sound commercial but just thought you'd wonder at the formality of the telegram & their prices here.

---

18 World Federation of Trade Unions.

19 With the freedom that resulted from the new constitution, trade unions blossomed. They had become powerful enough that they had planned a general strike for the first of February, in an attempt to take over factories. General MacArthur warned that he would not allow such a strike, and the unions relented, causing them to lose face and quieting them for the remainder of the occupation.

One thing I'm going to invest in here is a good camera. I've got my name on a list now to get one. I bought a G.E. light meter for it already. The light meter cost $15.25 at the PX. If you're ever around a camera shop at home, would you mind pricing them & letting me know how much they are there? I got the newest one G.E. put out & people tell me they're the best.

The traffic at 310 sounds as heavy as ever. It's so nice to hear of our friends, Mom. I am supposed to get that long lost check within the next few days. I'll send more silk & stuff then. So all can have a pair of P.J.'s. Am sending more pictures to Esther & Yvonne. They are to be cut in half & framed as a set. They mount them on mats & frame them with bamboo here. The artist will draw any flower in any color. If any of our friends want any certain flower or color, I'd be glad to get it for them. I thought maybe Mrs. Fansier would like one—she's been so nice about always remembering me.

I'm anxious to receive the package with the other clothes you bought for me. I certainly do appreciate your shopping & wonderful taste. Larry's suit sounds sharp. Bet it looks good on him.

Must close & practice my Russian alphabet. Thanks again to all of you for everything.

All my love,
Norma Jean

April 14, 1947

Dear Frances,

I received the gorgeous gloves in this morning's mail. Gee, I'm sure proud of them! They're really needed too as the weather is nippy enough yet to make it necessary for us to wear gloves most of the time. Thanks a million.

I got a letter from Dad this morning, too, telling me about his birthday celebration at the Cooney's barbeque. It sounded like lots of fun. Could I ever go for some of that Stateside food again. Our food is good, but the cook gets in a rut on certain things. He's been on an asparagus rut ever since I've been here. This week he's been all out for chili beans. Guess it's time for another food ship to come in.

Yesterday, we went to Euno Park in Tokyo & saw the cherry trees in blossom there. Trouble was, there were so many millions of Japanese there you could hardly see the trees. It was like Pershing Square, because on both sides of the street were soap-box speeches on politics. All the natives are excited about the election. The trees really were beautiful though. Lots of the Japanese had walked for miles & miles to see them & visit the shrines there. No allied personnel are allowed to go in the shrines.

We're having a little excitement at work now, as Colonel Murray will go on trial this week. He's the one who stole all the diamonds while at the Bank of Japan. Sure am glad I got there after he left. I'd rather be a spectator.

Must close as I'm on my lunch hour, & it's time to go back to work. Thanks again for the gloves, Frances. I really like them & they fit perfectly. Hope this finds the Cooney family all well. 'Bye now.

Love,
Norma Jean

April 15, 1947

Dearest Mom, Dad, Esther, & Larry,

I think I'm about the happiest gal in Tokyo tonight. I got two packages & lots of letters today. This morning, I received the darling shoes—they're perfect. I wore the brown ones back to work, & I forgot I had new shoes on; they were so comfortable. I love the color too. I have a pair of black ones, & I really needed some brown loafers. I now have the patent leather pumps on & they are just as comfortable. I think they're real sharp looking. I've been wishing they'd come by this Saturday, as I have a big date planned, & I needed some black dressy shoes to go with my good black dress I bought in New York—perfect timing—eh! Saturday night, I'm going to the nicest Officer's Club in Tokyo with my favorite Lt.

It was just like meeting an old friend to see the summer clothes that came in this afternoon's mail. My maid got just as excited as I did & kept saying "Mamasan?" "Papasan?" When I said hayee (yes) she said "nice—oo mamasan & papasan," which was the biggest understatement of the year. Right now, she's washing & pressing the dresses for "Jeansan."

Yesterday, I got the beautiful gloves from Frances. They certainly are nice—I really appreciate the wonderful knitting in them after my one knitting attempt.

I must tell you about my last weekend's experiences. Saturday morning, I had shots for Smallpox, Typhus, & Cholera. We have to keep taking them all the time. I felt swell after them & had a real exciting evening. Emilie & I were invited to General Casey's home for dinner. She went with his son, Lieutenant Casey, & I went with Gene Fitzgerald, a friend of the Casey family. He's a civilian & works for the Gov't. in Yokohama. They live in the most beautiful home I think I've ever been in. It has three floors, & many outside porches, which overlook the swimming pool in the garden below. It's very modern architecture & furnished beautifully. It belonged to a Japanese manufacturing big wheel before the war. They have very pretty maids & lots of them. They wear pretty kimonos all the time there. General & Mrs. Casey were at a party, but I met them when they came home. Oh, yes, their other son, Keith, who is a Corporal in the Paratroopers was also there. Really an interesting & nice family.

Sunday, Emilie & I went to Euno Park to see the Cherry trees in blossom there. It was a hot, dusty trip but the trees were beautiful.

April 16, 1947

I got interrupted & was unable to get back to my letter until this evening. Am very sleepy & tired so will just make this a shorty.

Thank you all very much for sending me such wonderful things. The Kleenex is really good to have again—the PX seldom gets any & then the dependants who don't have to work always beat us to it.

Goodnight for now.

Love,

Norma Jean

16 April 47[20]

Dear Esther,

Received the barrettes & combs. Thanks a million—really are useful as well as pretty. Am having lots of excitement at work now—a big inspection today. We've made headlines in the *Stars & Stripes* for three days now because of the trial.

Wish you could see our room as we have it fixed real cute now. Your beach trip sounds super.

Bye for now. N.J.

> *Colonel Edward Murray went on trial April 15, 1947 in a General Court Martial in Yokohama on charges that he misappropriated some $210,000 (in 1947 dollars) worth of diamonds and other precious gems while he was acting as custodial officer of the Bank of Japan. He had been arrested when he arrived in San Francisco Feb. 3, 1947. The Pacific edition of the "Stars and Stripes" for April 15, 1947 included the following two paragraphs regarding the trial. "Spectators in*

---

20 This was a postcard with Japanese writing on outside, a design of bird & bushes, & a five-cent Air Mail stamp.

the tiny courtroom sat breathlessly on the edge of their chairs as the king's ransom of unset gems was revealed by the prosecution. One envelope alone held 462 small diamonds.

"The larger stones, which range in size up to 18 carats, were contained in separate envelopes introduced as prosecution exhibit No. 1. The jewels were brought into court in a brown-paper wrapped cardboard box which had originally held photographic supplies."

April 22, 1947

Dearest Family,

Received Esther's swell letter & Mom's swell letter & the white sox this morning. I surely did enjoy the letters, & I like the sox. Have been thinking so much about you all lately—guess it was because I was a little under the weather. Friday, I felt awful, so stayed home. Emilie called the Dr., & he gave me lots of medicine. It included sulfa as my throat was infected. I stayed in bed Saturday & Sunday & went to work again Monday. I feel okay again—only a little weak. Also, I itch all over which is a reaction to the sulfa they say. And, I had such an exciting weekend planned. The Dr. said it was a good thing I got my bad throat stopped right at the start, as coughs, colds, etc. are terrific to get rid of over here, if you let them go.

You & your sunny weather talk. It's been rainy, windy & cold here this last week. Am so anxious for warm weather to come so I can wear some of these luscious clothes you've been buying for me.

As you can see by the money order, I finally got paid. I got $360.00 Mon., & I will get paid more in a few days. I hope you know how much I owe you. I know this money order will take care of only a small part of it but will send more later. I owe money to people here, also, which I can repay now. Everyone's always borrowing & lending as their payroll dep't is never on the ball.

Sure like the pictures you enclosed. Your hats & coats are so cute, Mom & Esther. Your bathing suit looks like a glamour job Esther—real sharp. Larry's suit looks very nice. Papasan looks good—guess your cooking still agrees with you, eh!

Yes Esther, I can get pearls here. Before I leave, I am going to get a strand of real pearls. They sell them in the PX for around $30-$40. They have lots of real, cultured & imitation pearls here. We're not supposed to buy real ones anyplace except the PX.

Mom, "san" on the end if a name is a honorific, or polite expression. The Japanese put it on everyone's name when speaking to them. Which reminds me—my maids were wonderful to me while I was sick. Hamako kept coming in, taking my pulse, bringing ice, or anything I wanted. Suemi was so cute. She brought her "friendo" in to see me & was delighted whenever she could get something for me. The second day, she brought me a present. It was a real pretty Japanese doll in a glass case. I really appreciate it, as I can tell it was from her own collection, because the ribbon around the case is old & the wood is well seasoned. Hamako speaks quite a bit of English but about all Suemi says is "Okay."

There are a few other things I'd like from Stateside. Bobby pins & black gloves. Also, I need a book for my Russian class. The teacher said any big bookstore in "New York or California" should have it. It is "Bondars Simplified Russian Method" 6th Edition Revised, Pitman Pub. Co.

When will Larry graduate? I'm anxious to hear about it & any plans he may have. Sure wish I could travel to C.O.P. for it.[21]

Thanks a lot Mom, but I don't think I'll need a charge account any place beside Bullocks.

What are you planning on doing on your vacation?

I don't know whether I told you about the trips they're offering us here or not. You go from Yokohama to Shanghai to Hong Kong to Manila & back in 23 days. It costs $210, which includes everything, as you use the ship as your hotel in port. A couple of trips have gone

---

21 College of the Pacific.

out already, & they'll be several a month later on. Emile & I want to go in September, as I'll have enough annual leave by then.

Must close as Emile had to work today & it's her lunch hour so will eat together. Bye now.

Love, Norma Jean

P.S. Our room looks so cute now. As soon as we get our pictures framed we're going to take some pictures to send home.

All our fish died except the first one we got. Since everyone died we put with him, we changed his name from Mike to B.O. Plenty.[22]

Must close & go to eat with Emilie. Hope your cold is okay, Mom.

Bye for now.

Love,

Norma Jean

P.S. Keep all the pictures I send unless I tell you differently. Got the Butterick Book. Thanks loads. I've already promised to loan it to three other girls—they're mad for them here.

April 24, 1947

Dearest Folks,

Just a line tonight to let you know I received that super package. Boy, the clothes are luscious. Have been trying them on several times. My room girl pressed them beautifully, which really makes them look sharp. The coat is just what I needed. I like the color very much, as it will go with many things & be good in almost any season. The Bembergs will be perfect for the hot, sticky weather everyone tells me we're in for. I just love the green eyelet two-piece, & it really fits swell. I think you made wonderful choices—you're super-duper shoppers.

Am feeling real good again. Have gone to bed early all week & have all my pep again.

---

22 Reference to a comic strip character.

Since I've led such a quiet life this week, there's not much to tell you. Am going to Yokohama tomorrow, as the PX there usually has the best silk selection. Will send some home soon.

I have lots of fun at work. There were three of us gals, but the Major didn't like one, so had her transferred. Our Col. is leaving for California next week, as his wife needs stateside hospitalization. Our new Col. is really a character—he never smiles, doesn't talk, but growls, & is a fiend for details & lots of inspections. Just hope he won't spoil our good deal there.

How does the phone strike affect things? I have an awful time keeping up with the news—the *Stars & Stripes* is usually gone by the time I get to the PX.

Must close for now. Thank you very much for sending & choosing these beautiful clothes—can hardly wait for hot weather so I can wear them.

All my love,
Norma Jean

P.S. (Sat. morn.) Am enclosing money order. Made it to Esther, as I thought she could cash it easier. My finances are sure a mess, yes?

April 29, 1947

Dearest Folks,

Received the package with all the wonderful things today. The shoes are really swell. Both pair fit perfectly. They are so comfortable as well as cute. I'm sure wild about the white eyelet bag—never have seen such a cute one. I noticed how easily it can be cleaned, too. The gloves are just what I wanted. Am supposed to go to a wedding Saturday. I can wear my new gloves & shoes & carry my new bag. One of the Lts. at the office is getting married here in Tokyo & we've all gotten invitations.

Sure like the other clothes you included. I was just thinking about that red jacket the other day & wishing I had it here. It was just like Christmas to open everything.

We've had more rain & lots of wind lately. Practically got blown off the sidewalk today.

Am all enthused about my work tonight. We had a meeting today where the Major told us what our future functions would be. I was sure surprised when he said I was to be the Accountant in the office. I have two G.I.'s & two civilian men, who are to work under me. Guess he got a load of my lousy typing & decided others would be better at that. It suits me fine. The boys & I have a good time together—they called me "Miss Accountant" all afternoon. If all goes well this will mean a raise for me after I'm here six months. Never thought I'd live to be an accountant. It beats me. Helen, the other gal, (she's an older woman) is to be Chief Clerk in charge of the correspondence, typing, etc. I'm sure lucky to be in such a swell set-up. Some people get stuck in some silly job the full term of their contracts.

We decided we needed refreshments, so they hired a Japanese who serves us coffee or tea at ten in the morning & at three in the afternoon.

Emilie & I are still studying madly at our Russian. It's hard but fun. Nearly everyone here goes to class at night. They make most of the G.I.'s. We go to Army School, which is just a block from us. They teach everything there from music to calculus. Lots of kids are getting high school & college credits for their work, as they are equivalent to them. We go twice a week at night.

Just got a phone call. One of my friends bought a projector for me today. All I need now is a good camera, which I should be getting soon too. I'll be all set to take color shots then. Will you please send me some Kodachrome color film or if you can't get that, some Ansco color film will do. The color shots are out of this world. When shown through the projector they look real enough to touch. You can also have prints made in color from the film.

Those newspapers you put in the package always look good to me. Never read the *Daily News* so thoroughly. By the way, could you send some of the *Life* magazines to me after you've read them? We only can buy *Life International* here, which leaves out a lot that the *Life* stateside includes.

Must close & study Russian. Thanks load & loads for sending me all those wonderful things.

All my love,
Norma Jean

Six

Dearest Folks,

It's Saturday morning & has been raining madly all night & morning. Am waiting to go shopping with Helen from the office so will just write a line while I wait.

Today is the wedding of the Lt. at the office. Poor guy has really been taking a beating from the other fellows. Three of us girls got together & got he & his wife a silver coffee pot & cake plate. The wedding is to be at 3 this afternoon at St. Luke Chapel, with the reception at the Officer's Club. They were married yesterday by the Japanese officials. It seems you have to be married by both to make it official with everyone. Sunday Morning—

Got interrupted yesterday & just now had a chance to go on with this.

Now I can tell you about the wedding. It was lovely. The bride was given away by her uncle, who is a Captain in the Navy. She had four bridesmaids. Three wore pale pink satin gowns, & the maid of honor wore pale blue. Her gown was really nice—white satin with a long train & a beautiful veil. Of course, all the grooms attendants were Army Officers, & they all looked so sharp in their dress uniforms. There was a large crowd at both the wedding & reception. At the reception, they had an orchestra & buffet snacks. They had a large cake, which they cut with a Japanese saber. Lots of flash & movie pictures were taken of the whole affair. The minister who married them was a Colonel friend of the groom & came from his station in Korea just for the wedding. They will spend their honeymoon at the beautiful resort hotel at Mt. Fuji. The whole affair was so nice, as no one got excited & everything went off so smoothly.

Col. Murray, the one who is on trial for stealing diamonds from the Bank of Japan, was in the office Friday. He's staying at the Grand Hotel pending the rest of the trial. He sat at the desk behind me. It was so exciting because lots of other Cols. came in & asked him questions, which will influence his case. He seemed to be a very nice person. He is very soft spoken & mild mannered. Poor fellow seems to have lost all his fight. Everyone doubts that they can prove he got the diamonds from here, but he'll be guilty of smuggling & actions unbecoming an officer. After he left, the Major called us together & said we should all be careful, as we're all probably being checked by the F.B.I. & Army Intelligence. Probably, they're checking our bank accounts now & will again after we return to the states. Don't know how I get into these situations, but golly it sure keeps life exciting.

I wore my new grey coat yesterday to the wedding. I got so many compliments on it, so I know it looked okay; it really is a good style & weight for lots of wear.[23]

May 3, 1947

Dear Mom, Dad, Esther & Larry,

I got your swell letter Mom & really enjoyed it. I also was awfully glad to get Larry's letter. I like the pictures you enclosed very much.

Have been working & playing hard all week. Now have four typists to dish work out to. The Major gives me orders & I give them the work. It seems all I do is answer questions all day. Just hope I'm giving the right answers, or I'll have to answer a few from the Col. We're working like mad to get the Vault Inventory Report out. But even under the present pressure, the boys & I have lots of fun doing

---

23 This letter ends here.

it. They all call me Jean. When the Col. comes in, the Major wants to sound dignified but never can remember my last name, so when the Col. is there I'm "Miss Jean." I really get a kick out of it.

Have an appointment for a perm. at the Old Kaijo Beauty Shop tomorrow morning. Am going to take my Japanese-English dictionary, so I can tell them not to cut my hair or that the machine is too hot.

Quite a situation developed with our maids last week. I came up from the dining room & saw a bunch of maids outside our door, & our regular maid was crying bitterly. Emilie was just leaving for the evening & seemed very unconcerned. I had them come in & between tears found out that Sumea (our regular maid) was crushed as Emilie had given some clothes to be pressed to the girl who had been her old maid. Sumea thought we didn't like her work. I tried in my best broken-English to explain the situation to her & her pals. She stopped crying, & I gave her some handkerchiefs for a present. I assured her she could have the pleasure of doing all our washing & pressing, & she once again beamed. The next day, she brought me a big bouquet. She's so bashful, she had to bring a friend with her to thank me for the handkerchiefs.

Did I ever envy you lucky people when I read that menu for Heyler's dinner—especially the strawberry short cake. The thing I miss most here is fresh milk—we never get it. They say we'll have it by fall however as they're going to bring some cows over then. We have fresh fruit everyday. We get apples & oranges for breakfast. We are allowed to buy tangerines from the natives, & they sure are good. We just dream about such things as bananas & strawberries.

I won't know the old neighborhood with the house across the street. How's it coming? Also—is Metricks still as good as it was? Gad, I'd buy the place out if I'd have a chance right now. The way this letter keeps going back to the food topic you can tell I haven't changed a bit. Guess I'll make myself a cheese & cracker sandwich.

I hope Larry comes out on top in the tests he took. Life at C.O.P. sounds exciting. Sure am glad he was able to live in such a nice place.

I got the letter that you forwarded from Dorothy Amon, Mom. Thanks. She wants to come to Japan & wanted info on how to do it. I answered the letter this evening. She lived at Rudy Hall & was Tiny's roommate.

Must close & eat that snack. Hope everyone at 310 is well.

All my love,
Norma Jean

May 12, 1947

Dearest Folks,

Just a line tonight to go with the money I'm sending home. We got paid today. If I can get to the P.O. on my lunch hour tomorrow will send a money order then.

It's raining again. It rained yesterday, last night, & all day today.

Saturday, it was quite nice, so Emilie & I played tennis at Meiji Park. Sunday, we went to the PX, & they had some play clothes. We both got some white shorts. They have plain shirts to wear with them. They're made of a sharkskin faille. We're lucky, because we couldn't try them on, & they fit us perfectly. Now, we're really set for some fancy tennis.

I spent most of my day Saturday in the Beauty Shop. I was there from 9:30 to 3 o'clock getting my permanent. They had to use all the curlers on the machine twice to get my hair fixed. Now it looks like so much fuzz, as I guess they cooked it too long. They ask you how long. Everyone around me said they thought about three minutes should do it. Guess it was too long. At least it should last quite a while. It isn't very short, as I wouldn't let them cut it at all.

I sure thought about you yesterday, Mom. Hope you had a very happy Mother's Day. Did you get the flowers? How is the telephone situation? I'd like to call home again. I think it's best not to on a holiday, as things are so tied up then, & they won't let you talk any overtime at all.

Am rather tired tonight, as we had an exam in Russian. He asked us ten questions in Russian, & we had to answer in our best Russian orally. Then we had to write five sentences in Russian. Next time we'll have a grammar quiz.

Love, Norma Jean

Seven

Dearest Mom, Dad, Esther & Larry,

I feel like a heel for not writing before. When I got your super letters today I decided I wouldn't go to bed without writing tonight. Have been enjoying the *Californian* very much—especially the background pictures of Long Beach.

The big Memorial Day weekend is over, & I'm just recovering.

I went to Mt. Fuji twice. It takes about three hours from Tokyo. It is really beautiful there. All different colors of Azaleas bloom everywhere. We saw Lake Hakon. There is a German colony there, & it looks like a typical European Chalet. The Germans are kept there while awaiting repatriation back to Germany. Many were colonists in the Dutch East Indies. The foliage on the hillsides was beautiful—all so green & pretty. There are lots of streams & small waterfalls. It was beautiful, but somehow rough roads & Jeep riding don't mix. I was practically eating off the mantel today.

Gee, I'm having such a swell time here. You just mention something & you get it. Everyone has been so nice to me. A Lieutenant friend of mine in Yokahama has a motorboat & access to a cruiser. Whenever Emilie & I feel like it, we call him up, & he takes us for a ride. We go down a river into Tokyo Bay. We plan to get our summer tans there this year.

Am enclosing a souvenir from the silk fair. It was held in a Jap. Dept. Store. None of the silk was for sale, but there was sure some beautiful material there. Also, an exhibit of how silk was made from the worm on up. They had a style show of western clothes & also a show of Jap. styles in silk. They had all Jap. models. In the Jap. show, they dressed the model as a bride & explained it as they went along. Sure was interesting.

I feel badly that your birthday gift will be late Mom. It's all ready to mail but I've been holding it, as no one knows the new duty rules & regulations clearly. Hope you had a nice birthday—just stay as sweet as you are.

Also—I missed youse guys anniversary, but I really thought of it—especially on the 29th. Have been gone on week ends, & the stores are all closed by the time I get out of work. I'm just not on the ball. Emilie's folks were married the day before you in Portland—the same year on the 28th. We decided that almost makes us relatives.

Was very glad to hear how I stand financially. I tried to have an allotment made to you, but they said that wasn't a very good idea, as they're so far behind in the payroll. They said it was best to send money orders home. I decided I'd send some home every payday. Take out all my bills, & the remainder will go toward the money I owe Esther & Mom from New York. When I get that caught up, just put it away for me or feel free to use it for anything you want, if needed. Have some more to send you now, but can't get to the P.O. to make out a money order.

Did you see in the papers about the outcome of Col. Murray's trial? He got 10 years at hard labor & was dishonorably discharged. The man looked so anemic when I saw him, I don't see how he'd last a year.

Hope you can all get to Larry's graduation. I think he has done so very well, & I sure enjoy his letters you forward.

I like your idea of buying things for me as you see them, as you always seem to know just what I want. This is really wonderful for me 'cause you know how I never was a shopping enthusiast. The fall suit idea is good. I have no particular choice of style but I'd rather not have a blue or grey one as my blue & grey ones are still good. Any other color will be okay.

The peonies are beautiful here now. Our maid brought us a big bouquet, & I was given a bouquet last week. Their flowers are very pretty here, but they don't have much of a smell. I had a corsage of red carnations, & it didn't smell at all. The wisteria is sure pretty now too.

Must close & put this aching back to bed. No more long Jeep rides for this kid for awhile.

Goodnight all.

Love, Norma Jean

P.S. I have a silk souvenir also, so do anything you want with this one.

June 11, 1947

Dearest Folks,

What exciting letters I've been getting from 310. That new car really makes me drool. I was so glad to get that picture of it. I'm so glad you got all the wonderful extras on it. I'm so numb from these rough roads & springless Jeeps that I wouldn't know how to act in our new car. I'm so glad you'll be able to go see Larry's graduation in it. That will sure be a nice trip.

Have been as busy as ever. Went to a formal dance at Yokohama Country Club last Saturday, & am going formal to the New Grand Hotel dance in Yokohama this Saturday. Emilie & Bill, & Gleason & I, are making a steady foursome lately. Gleason is very nice. He's a Lt. stationed in Yokohama. He may go to West Point & will know within two months. He's got the boats we go in & belongs to lots of nice clubs. In case you were wondering, Gleason is his first name— Coleman is the second. Most people think I'm calling him by his last name, when I say Gleason.

It seems to me its been raining since I've landed here. The rainy season started officially June 10th & is to officially end July 10th. It usually rains part of the day but is sunny & bright the rest of the day.

Sunday, it didn't rain until evening. Emilie & I took our first sunbaths of the season on the roof of Old Kaijo in the afternoon.

Got the songbooks in today's mail. The G.I.'s serenaded me all afternoon from them. They were really sharp on "Pistol Packin' Mama"—more fun.

As the weather is warming up, the mosquitoes are waking up. They put mosquito netting over all our beds. Everyone in our office had to go & get Encephalitis shots yesterday—no effects. We have to get more next week. After that I have to get more boosters for the other shots—what a life.

I meant to explain why I left the PX price list in the package, Mom. I just didn't want those customs officials to value the stuff too highly.

Am mailing a birthday package to you, Esther. Hope it makes it before July 1st, as the duty is going up then, & all packages will be held.

I just now thought of it—I landed in Japan just four months ago today—boy, has the time ever gone fast.

Your house redecorating sounds good. Your ideas for our room sound good Esther. Have you decided about the living room colors?

We saw "The Late George Apley" last week. I like to look in the picture ads in the papers from home to see the latest shows—we'll get them months from now. When people have just landed from the States, we always are eager to hear about the latest songs & shows. All our radio programs are about two months old by the time we get them.

Must close for now as I have a little sewing to do tonight.

Thanks for those super-duper letters & the music books. Sure will be thinking of all my wonderful family tomorrow—June twelfth. Have fun in the Nash.

P.S. How about some snapshots of you & the new car.

June 15, 1947

Dearest Family,

It's another rainy Sunday, & Emilie & I are really enjoying a quiet evening sewing & listening to the radio.

I received the package last Tuesday from home. I sure like the white slack suit, & it fits swell. I was very glad to get the bobby & hairpins. I liked everything you put in the box. I gave E. one of the tubes of shampoo, & we're anxious to use it. You are always so thoughtful.

Yesterday, I talked to Larry on the phone. Gee, it was so good to hear his voice again. I got mixed up & thought he graduated on the 12th. In his wire answering mine, he said to call Friday. I thought he meant Friday the 13th. It makes no difference, as long as I had such a good visit with him. It makes home seem so much closer when I know I can call & talk to you anytime. Just let me know when you want me to put a call through, & I'll be glad to.

We had a wonderful time at the formal dance at the Grand Hotel in Yokohama last night. I was very anxious to go there as Ruth Troy said she remembered that as being a very nice place & wondered if I'd been there. "We Four" were going sailing today in Gleason's new sailboat but had to postpone it because of the rain.

I have been sewing on the white dress you sent me tonight—shortening the length. I sure love it. Emilie has a cute white dress too, & we plan on wearing them next Saturday night, instead of formals, to the Bankers Club in Yokohama.

Work goes on as usual. We have a new Major, Capt., & Col. with us now, which means we'll probably get more G.I's & civilian personnel. Gad—now there are more officers than anything else swarming around the place. The Col. who left about a month ago was back to visit Friday. He talked to me quite a while, mostly about California, as that's where he spent his month's leave. He said prices were high & things still confused & that he was glad to be back in Tokyo.

Must make this a shortie as it's time to go to bed. Goodnight to all of you.

All my love,
Norma Jean

P.S. Sure enjoyed news from "The Firestone" & UCLA.
How's the Nash? You still have the Chevrolet I presume—really must be a sensation for Dad to drive the Nash then the Chevie.

June 26, 1947

Dearest Mom, Dad, Esther, & Larry,

Received the package with the shoes yesterday. I sure like both pair, & they fit swell. I love the style of both pair & can wear them with many of my summer clothes.

Have been busier than usual lately it seems. Emilie & I have been on another sewing jag. Today, we got the sewing machine we had signed up for in the PX two months ago. I have a peasant skirt already to stitch & will make a slip with eyelet lace to go with it. We're going to stitch & hem our bedspreads now too.

I sent your doll the first of the week, Esther. Sure hope it gets there okay. It is an old doll that came from Kyoto. The doll represents a court musician or entertainer. The instrument is wrapped separately in the box. Be careful as the little piece of bone is packed loosely with the instrument. It is the thing she plays with. Each fits into her hands when she's standing. Hope customs doesn't value her too high. It's awful, because we can't pay duty here—they just stop them all when they arrive in the states.

Sure have been thinking of what all of you are doing. How's 310 Larry? Will be anxious to hear your job plans & Esther's school plans.

The Army school is opening again. Emile & I are all set to continue Russian. We've got the book you sent & feel all set to go. We're all set to sew & ya-ta-ta in primary Russian for the next two weeks.

Summer is really here—the days are hot & sticky. Sure are getting a lot of fun wearing those lovely Bambergs you sent. The grey coat is never idle a weekend; it's swell to wear over formals, too.

Work is the same mad house—we keep getting more Colonels, Lt. Colonels, & Majors; they're practically stumbling over each other now.

They've changed my title again—now I'm officially Chief Clerk of the Accounting Section. It will probably be something else tomorrow.

Must close & start using the machine, as our days are numbered for its use.

Love,
Norma Jean

Eight

July 1, 1947

Dearest Folks,

Am on my lunch hour again. Was so glad to get Larry's swell newsy letter. His job plans sound very good. How did his new car deal come out? Sure hope he likes his work at Bakersfield.

Esther, the card from Catalina was darling. We had more fun with it at the office. We put it under a little notebook the Japanese coffee man keeps on his worktable. I engaged him in a "brilliant" conversation while Jim wound the fish up & hid it. When the coffee man went back we all watched & nearly died laughing. We thought he was going right through the floor. Poor "Joe" hasn't trusted us since.

How is Catalina? What happened to your & Yvonne's plans? By the way, I got an envelope with lots of jokes in it from her today. Am anxious to read them but decided I'd better not start here at the office, or that's all the GI's would be doing all afternoon. Sure have been thinking about you today as this is the day you said you were to start school. How's every little thing?

AEP school began again last night, & Emilie & I were right in there pitching at Russian class; we're going to beat that thing.

It's been raining again for the last three days. We were all set to go horseback riding Sunday—had our reservations & all—but couldn't because of the weather. Emilie & I got up early & went to church, ate lunch & shopped at the PX (it's open on Sundays), sewed in the

94

afternoon, then went to a concert in the evening. For a change, we actually got a lot of things done on a weekend instead of just playing around.

Larry mentioned in his letter that you stopped by Yosemite on your way home. How's dear old Camp Curry, the Lodge, etc?

Have a few things I would like from the States. Need some grip-tooth combs for my hair, Peds for my feet, & a peasant blouse for my new skirt I'm making. There's no hurry but just realized the need during the few hot days we had last week. Wow, it gets sooo sticky hot.

July 2, 1947

Dear Folks,

Here it is another day & I still haven't finished my letter. When I don't get a letter from home for a few days my morale is really affected, & Johnny at the office has to tell me to quit moaning. This morning, I received Esther's swell letter with the wallpaper & curtain samples. I really felt guilty for having not written home sooner but expecting so much from you.

We don't have to work on the 4ᵗʰ of July. Emilie & I are planning on taking in the huge parade & celebration in Tokyo Friday. Saturday we want to go to Nikko & Sunday to Karuiyawa if possible.

We have more fun with the two coffee men at work. Jim & Leonard taught them to sing "Shoo Fly Pie"—it's a scream because they're so serious & just love to sing it for anyone now. Today, they wanted me to teach them "You Are My Sunshine," which they practiced on madly all afternoon. They pronounce words so funny & never crack a smile while we all sit around knocking ourselves out.

Did you happen to read the article in *Colliers* (June 14 ed.) & *Newsweek* (June 23rd ed.) on Japan? They're quite popular reading here. The *Colliers* article is a little exaggerated but pretty good. The part about being able to take trips so much is wrong, as the dependents are coming before housing is ready, & they occupy all the rest of the hotels while waiting for housing.

>*The "Colliers" article includes some pictures of a dance hall, a skating rink, and other places where G.I.s could entertain Japanese women. The two paragraphs quoted below also summarized how apparently the American occupiers were living and working.*
>
>*"Aside from the G.I., who has it good enough by anyone's overseas standards, most of the Americans live in the best parts of whatever region they occupy, possessing the best private houses, the best of the relatively few hotels and apartment buildings thoughtfully left around by the B-29 boys, or the spanking new Quonset cottages and houses put up by the Army with Japanese labor. The highest price even a general can pay for a mansion complete with Army-furnished heating systems, refrigerators, furniture and five Japanese servants: $100.50 per month, the maximum in the War Department scale. The average: closer to $51.*
>
>*"The heart of the American capital is the mile or two of modern office buildings and hotels miraculously spared by the B-29s, an oasis of solidity and comfort in the burned or blown-out wreckage of Tokyo's 'missing' buildings. It stretches roughly from the Imperial Palace, upon which General MacArthur can look down from his marble offices in the great Dai Ichi Building to the Ginza, and up and down 'MacArthur Boulevard,' and weaves across occasional ruins to include scattered smaller cases of London-like office buildings or hotels."*
>
>*The June 23rd issue of "Newsweek" she cited was highly critical of General MacArthur and the*

economic policies that had been developed. Later in 1947 many of these policies were reversed as the goal of the United States became making Japan a partner and a strong Asian bedrock.

I'd sure like to see our room after you finished, Esther. It sounds sharp—I love the colors you chose.

Will be glad to get the blouses you mentioned in your letter of today. When it's handy would you send Emilie & me some Anatole Robbins make up, as they just have Max Factor in the PX.

Must close & study a little Russian before bedtime. Will be anxious to get Larry's new address.

Love, to all,
Norma Jean

July 5, 1947

Dearest Folks,

Have been sunbathing on the roof with Emilie, had a shower, & am now resting until dinner. It's a lovely day—nice & warm with a cooling breeze. We went to the PX this morning & had a swell rickshaw ride back.

Yesterday was a big day in Tokyo. We had a parade to end parades. Troops of all the Allied powers were in it. About the most colorful were the Indians. They wore turbans, kilts & played bagpipes, flutes, & drums. Took a lot of pictures, which I will send, if they come out good. MacArthur, Eickelberger, & all the wheels were there. Emilie went with a foreign correspondent & sat in the reviewing stand near Mac & the wheels. All afternoon & evening, she attended teas, buffets, & dinners. Leave it to me, I had a stomachache all day so canceled my afternoon & evening dates. Feel swell again today—guess it was something I "et." We were supposed to go to Karuiyawa today, but neither of us woke up in time but really had a good time right here in Tokyo. They had a big air show this morning. It was really something—never saw so many planes all at one time. It really seemed to impress the natives as they sure took it all in. Tomorrow, we plan on going to Yokusuka (pronounced Yo`kuska) to see & take pictures of the Army transport ship that went aground.

July 3rd I received the package with the white blouses & gloves. They're really swell & much needed. My blouse situation was really critical, as I kept waiting & waiting but the PX still hasn't gotten any in. These will be just perfect for this sticky weather. Sumeasan pressed them & they really look nice. They fit just right, too. Thanks loads & loads.

Emilie & I have found another new interest. We went to a meeting of L.A.R.A. (Licensed Agencies for Relief in Asia). When we came away, we had been appointed as the publicity committee. Our duty is to try to get more publicity for LARA in the states. Protestant churches through the World Christian Service Fund, the Catholic Church, C.I.O. A.F. of L, & a couple of other organizations contribute funds for LARA. It is sure swell, as I will get some very good experience & material & so will Emilie, as she's gathering material for a thesis on Far East Foreign Relations. The lady in charge of it lives at Old Kaijo, too. She sure is interesting. She was presented to the Emperor about a month ago for her outstanding services in LARA.

Gad, between Russian class, LARA, dates, athletics & sightseeing we're really a couple of busy bees.

Must close for now as it's time for dinner then a show.

'Bye for now.

Love,
Norma Jean

July 8, 1947

Dearest Family,

Received your most wonderful letter yesterday, Mom & have really enjoyed reading it several times. It was so good & newsy. I was so thrilled to hear about Larry's new car & job. Things are changing fast at 310.

It's sticky hot all the time now. We sure make good use of our mosquito netting at night, as the bugs drive you to insomnia without it. Sure am enjoying the summer clothes & shoes you sent me.

Am enclosing some color pictures Lou took of me. They were taken in about March. The one where I'm with the Japanese women was taken at the main entrance gate of the Imperial Palace. The natives just love to have their pictures taken & will pose at the drop of a fan. A crowd usually gathers to take it all in. The little house you can see part of with the Cavalry Insignia is the guardhouse for Allied Nations. No Allied personnel are allowed to go in past this entrance, but Japanese go & bow before the Emperor's Palace. The picture of me sitting down was taken on the Inner moat of the Palace Ground—just about a block from Old Kaijo Hotel. The picture taken in the street was in Chinatown at Yokohama—it was a rather cold day so I borrowed Louis' leather jacket. Keep these pictures, as I have the films I show in my projector.

So glad Esther had such a happy birthday; the watch sounds sharp.

Your trip to Yosemite sure brought back memories of two summers ago. You certainly saw & did a lot of things on your Stockton trip.

Hate to stop now, but I have to shower & get dressed. Am going to see Marie Coughlin (the girl I met on the ship) & her boyfriend tonight. He got some new records from the States & wants me to hear them tonight. Am going with a fellow who is a photographer with the R.A.F. that Earl (Marie's boyfriend) introduced me to—wow, what a sentence!

In haste—
Love,
Norma Jean

July 20, 1947

Dearest Mom, Dad, & Esther,

Sure have been enjoying your letters. Felt a little guilty about having told you of not getting mail as I do realize how busy you all are—especially at this time. And letters really take the time.

Emilie & I just got back from the PX. They had everything today. Even oriental rugs—they cost from $100-$200, but they were just scrumptious. I bought a Chinese silk slip ($5), a beautiful scarf ($1) & some rayon yardage (35¢), plus our usual candy & gum ration.

By the way, our payroll is seven weeks behind so am constantly broke & unable to send any home. At least I'll have a lot saved when I quit here. A lady was at work Friday to re-classify us & give us better ratings. It will take a while, but a raise is definitely in sight now. Emilie & I are both trying to save $2000 for our European trip so we're being very angelic at work now.

Got a nice letter from Larry, & one from Kathryn Cullmer. At last, I wrote to Clarice today & sent two cute charm bracelets to Esther & Gladys Strobel. By the way Esther, am getting a good collection of bracelets. Am going to bring them home as my personal belongings, so no duty. Have a rose quartz charm bracelet, enameled silver charm bracelet, bone skull heads bracelet, identification & several silver ones.

Mom, am sending you a pair of ivory earrings. I wore them, but they keep breaking. Their solder & workmanship is so inferior; I can't get them fixed here, so I thought you could get them fixed & wear them.

It sure seems funny not to have you at the P.O. Esther but I do think your school is a grand idea. I know how you feel about Spanish. E. & I are still battling it out with Russian.

We went to church this morning. I wore my aqua eyelet white straw hat (PX) I just love that dress & those accessories. Otherwise, nothing too new has been happening. We play tennis on lighted courts at evening time now. Also, we see shows at the Outdoor Theatre. The weather is glorious at night now.

Must close for now.
All my love,
Norma Jean

July 23, 1947

Dearest Family,

Received both packages this week. The sweaters look hot now, but they will sure be nice this winter. I like the colors & styles very much. The magazines & papers have been well read & are being loaned out now. The bathing suit is scrumptious & fits like a glove; Emilie says "It's a sharpie." Sure like the blouse, & it is just what I wanted for my peasant skirt. It's the cutest blouse of that type I've seen in a long time.

Am on my lunch hour now—wow, is it ever hot. Have been wearing the white jersey blouse you sent me for Christmas, Esther, as it's nice & cool.

Emilie & I haven't been doing too much lately—too hot for much action. We do go swimming & play tennis on lighted courts at Meiji Park, when we get the energy.

Received a swell letter from Larry this week. He sounds very happy with his work. I got a big "charge", as he calls it, from his description of working with his Okie clients.

The boys are all coming back from lunch so better cut this short.

Got a minute, so decided to carry on. Things must have quieted down at 310 now with the company & all gone. Now you can really enjoy your clean & redecorated house.

A couple of weeks ago Emilie & I ordered bicycles from Montgomery Ward in Oakland, Calif. It's impossible to rent them in Tokyo, & they really come in handy here. The locals use them all the time. We are going to rent them out when we're not using them & by the amount of kids that say they want to rent them, we expect to be repaid for them in a short time. We're still planning on bicycling through Europe & decided we'd get in form now. Also, when you go to visit places here on the train, there's no transportation when you get there. So, we're planning on taking our bikes with us. We're just hoping they can fill our orders. They cost forty dollars including shipping costs. We can keep them in the baggage room at Old Kaijo. It's too hot to do much riding now, but they'll be wonderful in the fall.

I don't know whether I told you or not, but Emilie expects to go home in October for a visit. She hasn't been home for 27 months now, & her folks are getting anxious to see her again. Sure hope she has a chance to go to California so she could meet you all. She said she may take a trip there with her folks. She's quite the kid. We're both so thankful that we just happened to be roommates, as there are so many characters living here. Most of the girls are older than we are, it seems.

The clock says it's quitting time so I'd better stop or get paid time & a half for this.

'Bye for now—
All my love,

Norma Jean Cone
Civilian Employee
TKMGD, Bank of Japan
P.S. Got a letter from Montgomery Wards—no bicycles, so we got our money back.

Sunday evening
July 27

Dear Folks,

Was cleaning out my purse & found I'd forgotten to mail this letter. Have had a nice weekend. Friday evening, I ate at one of the dependant's home. That home cooking sure tasted good. They have such cute homes & everything (linen, silver, maids, & houseboys) is furnished. Saturday, I played tennis in the evening then went to the Yokohama Country Club. This morning, Emilie & I went to the PX. We each bought some Chinese brocade & jade rings. The rest of the day we've just been trying to keep cool. Must close & start fanning again.

N.J.

July 30, 1947

Dearest Folks,

Sure did like the letters from home. They were so good & newsy.

Tom Neal, a G.I. in our office, left today for the replacement center to be sent home, as his time is up. He's planning on going by way of Calif. & said he'd drop in to see you folks. He's an awfully nice kid. He's from Indiana & wants to go back to college. I gave him your address & phone number. He's very large & quite bashful, so it would help if you remembered his name when he calls. I do hope he will call when you're home. It will probably be a month before he'll get there. I told him to take a ride in our new car & tell me about it.

Emile said her father's office address is 1110 3rd Ave., Seattle. Her mom lives on Vashon Island. But we both thought it would be best to see her Dad, as it's much easier to get to him, & he can take you to the Is. depending on your plans. We'd both appreciate your getting together, as we think we have the best parents Stateside. If you've forgotten, his last name is Graf.

Our hot weather was broken with rain today, & it sure feels good. The typhoon season is next, which everyone seems to rather enjoy here—lots of wind & rain I gather.

Must close & go to "Chow."
Norma Jean

P.S. #1 Sure like the clippings you sent.
P.S. #2 Even prune short cake sounds good!

Nine

Dearest Family,

I've just finished work & am waiting for Helen so decided to take advantage of my spare time. Am sweltering in the meantime. Also, am eating a box of cookies a GI gave me.

Got the wonderful package in yesterday's mail. It came through just perfect. The blouses are darling—am planning on wearing the pink one tomorrow night at the American Club. Sure was glad to get the Peds, make-up, & Kleenex.

Wednesday afternoon, I got off work to take a driving test for a Jeep license. Haven't heard whether I passed or not but doubt it very much. How was I to know where you should park a convoy, how fast a convoy was to go at night & at day, or if the air filter had anything to do with the crankcase? We had fifty questions such as that, then had to pass reaction, sight, depth perception, & color blindness tests. It was a lot of fun anyway, & we got a nice refreshing ride & afternoon off out of the deal. I was the only girl taking the test, but most of the fellows were ones I knew from our detachment. Thank goodness we didn't have to take a road test as I've never driven a Jeep in my life.

Yesterday, got all excited as the first typhoon was supposed to strike. It drizzled the night before off & on. At noon, it just poured, & at four o'clock the wind began to blow. Then, the rain stopped, & the wind ceased; by seven o'clock, it was as hot & sticky as it's been all week.

The paper had kept warning us all week of "Gwen" the typhoon, & we were frankly disappointed when it shifted its course. The hotel even had emergency lighting ready.

Emilie & I are still struggling with Russian. Last night, the teacher said we should be able to speak it within a year, but we're convinced that two years will be our minimum. About forty started the class, & now there are only ten of us left. It's kind of fun—not much grammar but mostly conversation.

Tomorrow I'm going to get material to write two case histories for a booklet Emilie & I are working on for LARA. We'll send you an autographed copy, when we get it printed. It is going to all the organizations in the States that contribute to LARA. There still is a lot of work that has to be done before "we go to press".

Am trying to get annual leave, so Emilie & I can take a trip to Northern Japan this month, but the Captain says no. There's been such a turnover in the office that he said no one could be freed to take over my duties. We'll go in Sept., I guess. Would I ever love to join your campfire in Kern River!

Helen is just about ready to go, so must close. 'Bye now.

Love, Norma Jean

17 September 1947

Dearest Folks,

Am again on my lunch hour. We eat at the Riverview Hotel, as it's only two blocks away from the Bank, & we scarcely have time to get to our billets & back in our lunchtime.

Received your wonderful letter, Mom. Sure was glad to get the details of your vacation. You & Dad sure got around. It's too bad you didn't have more time.

I just remembered that you asked me what WDC stands for. It's for War Department Civilian. Civilians over here are known as either a WDC or a Dependant.

It's really gorgeous today. The sky is clear blue, the sun is shining brightly, & there is just enough of a cool breeze to make you feel full of pep. Monday, "Kathleen" (a typhoon) was supposed to come. It rained all day & about six o'clock all the lights went out. It rained madly, & the wind blew a little. It was exciting but we were again disappointed, as it was just a slight typhoon. It seems that "Kathleen" also detoured Tokyo at the eleventh hour. All the Allied buildings have emergency lighting for such occasions, but that is limited to hallways & lobbies. Emilie & I took a ride on a bus to see how the rest of Tokyo was doing. It was completely blacked out. We had lots of fun as we decided to put on some crazy old clothes, as the rain was really heavy. We also put on gatas--Japanese wooden shoes. They're wonderful for such weather as the rain goes right down your goulashes anyway. We wore no socks, but the weather was not cold, so we didn't get a bit cold. The natives sure got a charge out of seeing American girls wearing gatas. Speaking of rain, etc., I was wondering if you could send me some white boots for this winter. Everyone says they're the best things for snow around Tokyo in the winter. My galoshes are about shot, & they are not good for much. I mean the white rubber rain boots that they wear in California. Don't need any more clothes. Am going to wear out what I have so won't have so much to pack later—it's hard to realize I've been here seven months already.

The PX is expanding a lot, so they will have a larger variety of things they say. I bought a maroon leather makeup case last week there. It was just $9. It is very well made & has a mirror inside it. Most of the girls have them here, as they are perfect for overnight trips. Am planning on sending Esther some money for luggage as I have hers, & she must be needing some now. Sure will be thinking of her next week.

20 Sept '47

Dear Folks,

Have been carrying the other letter around & haven't had a chance to finish it. It's Saturday morning, & Emilie is at work.

Received such a nice letter from Esther yesterday.

Tomorrow, Emilie & I are planning on going to the flood area. You've probably heard about the flood in central Japan. We're going in a truck that belongs to LARA. Will probably take some relief supplies with us. We want to take pictures, too.

Thursday, the Major called me in; he said he was sending me to Yokohama for the afternoon. He was very mad, because we were supposed to get our raises long ago. When he called about it that morning, they said they had no one to make out the forms. He said he'd send me down, so ther'd be no more hold up. Soo—I went to Yokohama & wrote up my own promotion. I'm getting a raise from $2442 to $2710 a yr.

Am enclosing a few pictures we took on our vacation at Noboribetsu.

Must close & get to the PX.

Love,
Norma Jean

24 Sept. 1947

Dearest Mom & Dad,

Imagine Esther is in San Jose now. Will be anxious to hear from her & get her address there.

'Twas payday today, so will enclose $20 M.O. Am not sure how much or to whom I owe money but decided that I'd send it home while I had it. Would appreciate a statement from you on how much to send. I don't think I've ever sent any for my insurance either, so be sure & add that. When I get caught up, I want to send some for you to have for things that may arise. The Bank of America is opening a

Branch Office here next month so will open my account there—still have my bankbook from them at home ($5 bal.).

Last Sunday Emilie & I went with the LARA group to the flood area north of Tokyo. The M.P.'s stopped us at one of the bridges, so we didn't get too close. Japanese & U.S. Army trucks were constantly crossing, loaded with people & their belongings. Many were walking & had huge bundles tied on their backs. The Japanese Red Cross was directing the sick, weary, aged, & injured. One of the fellows we were with spoke fluent Japanese, so he translated for us. It was pitiful to see the old people walking such great distances with their meager possessions strapped to their backs. Heaven only knows where they'll all go or what they're going to eat, as conditions are really rugged for them in the crowded Tokyo area.[24]

Just as I got WDC explained to you they change it—just like this Army. Now we're D.A.C.'s—meaning Department of Army Civilians. It just went into effect last weekend.

Northwest Airlines just opened an office in Tokyo. It's across the street & down half a block. Will enclose one of their schedules from here.

Hate to make this so short but must go eat dinner—am just famished.

All my love,
Norma Jean

---

24 According to the Asian Disaster Reduction Center (ADRC), Typhoon Kathleen brought the greatest flood damage to the Kanto region. The damage was especially horrible in Tokyo & Saitama prefectures and in the Tone River basin. There were 1,930 killed or missing, 1,751 injured, 292,455 hectares of fields inundated, and 390,041 houses flooded.

28 September, 1947

Dear Mom & Dad,

It's Sunday afternoon & am listening to the Cal-Navy football game. Emilie & I went to church this morning & have just finished lunch.

Dad, I sure thought of you yesterday & wished you could have been here to help Emilie & me rummage through the dump. You'd have had a field day. During the war, the Japanese Gov't had a brass drive, & there are now the Brass Dumps from these drives. There is one about four miles out of Tokyo. We took a bus part way & walked about two miles. We had to get a special pass from the Provost Marshall's office to get in, as they are Off Limits. It covers about a block & is piled high with all kinds of brass junk. It was so funny to see everyone digging through it. There were quite a few high-ranking Army officers & their wives digging for all they were worth—& they made a racket. We wore our old slacks & soon got into the spirit. Lots of the good stuff has been taken, but there are millions of altar candlesticks, coins, etc. I got candlesticks, coins, an old fork, & some beat up medals. All evening, Emilie & I polished our brass. We both have blisters on our fingers this morning. I only have ½ of 1 candlestick shining as it's quite a mess. I got one pair of candlesticks about 10 inches high of which I'm going to have lamps made. They're real cute as they have Elephant heads & tusks for handles. I think they came from a temple as there were so many with the same design out there. If you can find some good brass polish or stuff to put on it to keep it shiny, will you please send me some? We might go back again, as we've got the system now. You should wear gloves, jeans, & take a digger. They have some altar candles about two feet high that match mine, which people were taking to make ashtrays out of. Which also reminds me—would you please send my old jeans & plaid shirts? Will enclose a couple of coins straight from the dump.

It's a gorgeous day. The air is a little chilly, but the sun is shining beautifully. The Nips are all playing baseball madly, the WAC's had a parade yesterday, the Australians had one this morning, & the Yanks are rushing around in Jeeps stopping only to take more pictures.

By the way—Mrs. MacArthur sat right in front of us at church this morning.

One of our room girls, Homako, & I were talking the other night. We were listening to some music, so I asked her what songs she liked. She wouldn't sing unless I joined in. The only songs we both know are "Auld Lang Syne" & "Onward Christian Soldiers", so we sing them together all the time now—she in Japanese & I in English. She's a Methodist also so knows several hymns.

Must close for now & polish my brass some more.

Love,
Norma Jean

29 Sept. 1947

Dear Larry,

Enjoyed your last letter so much. Are you still working for your room & board?

Will enclose some pictures taken on our vacation in Hokkaido. Will you please send them to the folks after you're finished?

We haven't gone on any trips since our vacation but have been busy just keeping up with our usual routine. We're still taking Russian twice a week & are doing volunteer relief work for Licensed Agencies for Relief in Asia.

Yesterday, Emilie & I went to the brass dump about four miles out of Tokyo. It was brass donated by the people to the Gov't during the war. We've been madly polishing our candlesticks we got there last night & today. I meant to ask you if you like silk shirts. If you do, tell me what style & size, & I'll have some made for you at the PX. They only charge $1.50 to make them. If you would like some, it might be best to send an old shirt, as its hard to make them understand sometimes. Also, tell me what color you'd like.

My work goes on about the same. Last week was rough as both my typists were gone. The fellow was in the hospital, & the girl was taking the Major's secretary's place, as she was stranded in Northern Japan in the flood. A couple of G.I.'s & I carried on but not in very good style. Friday they hired a Japanese National typist. She can't speak a word of English, so I imagine I'll have loads of fun trying to explain to her what to do. I like my job, but Social Work is sure more interesting & satisfying than trying to please Army brass. Think I'll join your profession again as soon as I hit the States. Am I ever thankful to have my degree & experience. Most of the girls here will have to get a job typing for about $25 a week, when they go home. I got a raise this month & am making $2710 a year now.

How's the car? It must really be a pleasure to make long home hauls in it. Your mileage & meal rates sound good.

Must close for tonight Larry. Will try to answer your most welcome letters more promptly after this. Hope this finds you feeling tops.

Love,
Norma Jean

Ten

Dearest Folks,

Am at work, & everybody has gone but three of us Civilians. Sure seems quiet without the Army yelling around.

Have been knocking myself out the last two days trying to explain work to two Japanese girls who can't speak a word of English. I have an English-Japanese Dictionary, & they have Japanese-English ones, so we really have some rare conversations. The Major said they were mine to train & have work done, so I keep myself busy thinking up things that will be easy to explain. So far, they've been typing reports that consist mostly of columns of figures. But, they have an awful time with the word headings. I can imagine how awful it would be to type a language you couldn't even read. They are both real tiny & bashful & about fall off their chairs when the Major comes over & kids them. Yesterday, the Major bought some ice cream & cookies to go with our coffee. They sure liked it.

Monday morning, when I came in to work everyone had heard about my trip to the dump, as I had seen Capt. White out there. I was really surprised when the Col. came over & asked me what I had gotten. He said Capt. White told him that the last time he looked over my way all he could see was the top of my head above the piles of brass. The Col. is such a nice, dignified old man that I didn't know what to expect. Then, he proceeds to tell me about the time his wife went to the big dump at Nagoya. He said I should wear old clothes, gloves, & take a digger—also he said to take some cigarettes & candy, as the Nips will get some good stuff for you in an exchange. He also told me how to polish brass the easy way. He said to take vinegar & concentrated lemon powder & let it stand in that about an hour. Capt. White is getting me some of that so I'm really set now. I do need something to put on it to keep it shiny tho, & the only thing they could think of was colorless nail polish. I was wondering if you had found anything for that.

Last night, we had the formal opening of the dining room at the Old Kaijo Hotel. It was sure nice. We had candles, flowers, a stylish & wonderful meal & all the waitresses wore matching blue kimonos. We had tomato juice or soup, shrimp cocktail, ham or steak, peas, potatoes, asparagus, lettuce or Jell-O salad, fresh parker house rolls, tea or coffee, & for dessert our choice of ice cream, cream puffs, chocolate éclairs, or French pastries. They had a huge cake made in the shape of the Old Kaijo Hotel. The waitresses all looked cute as could be in their kimonos & with their hair piled up on their head.

Wed. Evening.

Didn't have time to finish at work. We've had dinner & are listening to the Alan Young show.

Have a slight cold, so will go to bed early tonight.

Mom, could you send me a couple plain, white, cotton or Rayon, sport blouses? I need some to wear with my sweaters to work this winter. So far, they've never had any at the PX.

Must close for tonight & get to bed.

Love,
Norma Jean

2 October 1947

Dearest Esther,

Was sure glad to get a letter from you today. I noticed the darling stationery first thing.

It must have been terribly hard for you to make the decision to go to school. Dave certainly has been nice to you & the folks. In her last letter, Mom told of how thoughtful he always was. It probably is best that you did go, as it will help you decide for sure how you want things. All I want for you Esther is happiness. I was so glad you said you were feeling okay, as I sure wonder about you. Emilie is swell, but no one can take my wonderful sister's place.

Nothing too new has been happening around Tokyo. Everyone's getting letters asking about the flood & typhoon.

Must tell you about my latest heartthrob. He's an officer who works in our office—tall, dark, & handsome. He just found out today that he's now a Major, so he & I are going to celebrate tomorrow night at the American Club. He's a wonderful dancer, & we have a good time together. Fun while it lasts, but he won't be here long—that's the Army for you.

Am sending a little package to you. Hope you can use it. Don't think there will be duty on it.

Must close as it's time to go to Russian class—hate to go tonight, as I haven't studied all week.

All my love,
Norma Jean

1 November 1947

Dearest Larry,

At last have a little time to write you—don't know how I keep so darn busy. Enjoyed your letters immensely & intended answering long ago.

Have been wanting to tell you about a most interesting person Emilie & I know. Two weeks ago, we were invited to visit our friend, Mrs. Sohma, at her summer home in Karuiyawa. It is a five-hour train trip from Tokyo. We met her on the eight o'clock train Sat. morning. She has a special privilege pass to ride on Allied trains, as her father is in the Japanese Parliament. She made the trip very interesting, as she pointed out things along the way. We went through the worst of the flood area. She said it was a terrible loss, as it would take many years to reclaim the soil. When we got to Karuiyawa, we ate at the Mampei Allied Hotel, as we're not allowed to eat in Japanese homes. In the afternoon, we rode two of her bicycles all around the village. We were so tired after our trip & bicycling that we didn't have the energy to walk to dinner at the hotel. We sat by a big fireplace & she fixed us tea, toast, & blueberry jam. We had brought some cheese & meat spreads, so we sat around a low table on the floor by the fire & had a wonderful time. She & Emilie knitted, & I kept the fire roaring. Mrs. Sohama talked most of the evening, & Emilie & I were practically spellbound. Her mother was half English, & she was raised with a very liberal attitude. Her mother worked with Episcopalian missionaries before her marriage. Her father, Mr. Ozaki, was always in politics—he was the outstanding liberal of Japan, & still is. He was exiled for one year because of his views just before the war. The family lived in England for that year. They traveled also to the U.S., Continental Europe, & India. They were very wealthy & were always entertained by foreign diplomats. Her stories of the Japanese police spy system, etc. were very interesting. I was surprised as the police gave her father protection all the time from his rivals, & at the same time constantly spied on him. She said they never interfered with his activities until the war actually started. During the war she & her husband & four children were sent to the Manchurian occupation. She said it was cold & bleak there. Besides her four children, she also is keeping two children whose parents were killed in Manchuria. Some of her friends' husbands from there are being held by the Soviets. During the war, Karuiyawa was a big colony for the Germans. Most were repatriated by the 15ᵗʰ of Aug. this year, but a few are still there. She said she couldn't get along with them, so she just ignored them. She's now working for the "Readers Digest" in Tokyo. She translates & helps edit the Japanese edition. She & her husband live with another family in three rooms of a bombed out hospital in Tokyo. The servants care for the children & they make that long trip almost every weekend. They have two lovely homes there. Emilie & I stayed in a large guesthouse at night. It's wonderful for the children as the scenery is beautiful there, & they can have dogs, cats, & run all over the hills. Before the war, two of the American diplomats used to vacation at their place. Colonel Lindberg also stayed there on one of his visits in Japan. Mrs. Sohma is now heading a Social Reform movement for Japanese women. She's rather discouraged as she says the women don't know how to use their independence. The family has always been the influencing factor & now they completely lack any feeling of social responsibility. For instance their veterans' hospitals are in a terrific state. She says the men's morale is terribly low as they feel forgotten. The Allies will not even allow reading material sent to them. She's afraid Communism will spread like wildfire once it gets started—& it is getting a good hold here now. MacArthur is doing okay as far as he's going, but everyone has the feeling it could, & should, be extended down to the common people a lot more. Last week, I saw two Communist labor party rallies from the window at the bank.

About ten o'clock, we heard a Jeep outside—it was the M.P.'s; we had our special authority to stay in a Japanese home so just showed them that. We don't know how they knew we were there. It gives you a good feeling though, as you have that wonderful feeling of good old U.S. protection. They said they had orders to check on all Americans in Japanese homes that night. We went to bed soon after that & left about noon the next day.

Must close for now Larry, as I'm going for a short trip to Ohta (about fifty miles) this afternoon & must get ready. Will be glad to hear more of your stateside activities again.

'Bye for now,
Love, Norma

P.S. Note the change of address--faster this way

10 November 1947

Dearest Folks,

Am at the Mampei Hotel in Karuiyawa this weekend. We have a holiday tomorrow so took Monday off too. We left Tokyo Saturday morning & will return tomorrow afternoon. Six of us came together. John & Emilie came in the LARA truck with the supplies for an orphanage near here. The rest of us (Helen, Ted, Carl & myself) came in Ted's 1947 Chevrolet. We've had lovely weather—clear but rather cold due to the altitude. We arrived Sat. afternoon, had lunch, then went to the orphanage. It is a Methodist Mission for homeless children. We brought them flour, sugar, soy, etc., which is to last them for the winter. They were very nice to us. The children sang songs, & they wanted us to sing with them. They had learned "Jesus Loves Me" in English & were proud to sing it with us. Ted & John both speak Japanese fluently, so its been much more interesting than usual.

We're staying at Mr. Eisenberg's home here. It's a real large place. He's a Polish national who has married a Japanese woman. He owns a lot of factories & is somewhat of a wheel. We girls have the bedroom with the "kutatsu". We sleep on the floor, Japanese fashion, with a mat under you & a real thick quilt over you. The caretakers fix the kutatsu every evening. It is a big hole in the floor in which they put hot coals. A wooden frame is over this with blankets over that. It keeps your feet warm all night. We also have been initiated into the regular Japanese bath. You wash thoroughly, then get into a big, round wooden tub filled with very hot water. This is called the O-furo. Last night, we had a big Sukiyaki dinner at Mrs. Sohma's. We brought the food & she fixed & served it. It is hot rice with grilled beef, onions, cabbage & other vegetables over it. Yesterday morning we all went to Kuratsu Hot Springs--a three-hour train ride from here. This morning, we went bicycling & horseback riding. We're just recovering this afternoon.

Tonight, we're going to have a wiener roast around the fireplace. We eat at the Hotel when we want to & cook at the house other times. Will finish this later—time for ping pong now they tell me.

Thurs. evening—

Arrived back to Tokyo Tuesday evening & have been so busy that I couldn't put the finishing paragraph on the letter I started. We sure had a swell time in Karuiyawa. Got to be quite the experts with chopsticks—more fun!

Mom, I got the package with the jeans & blouses just before I left last week. Boy, does it ever feel good to get into my old jeans & shirt. The white blouses are just wonderful & were much needed. I wear sweaters, blouses & skirts all the time to work now. Will try to get a tea set sent home soon. They have lots of them. Might get one at the PX if they have some nice ones now. The whole occupation is groaning as it's inoculations time for everybody again. We have them in November & May. Today, I had Smallpox, Cholera, & Typhus shots. The whole office force was called in at the same time.

Have my Christmas box about ready. Will try to mail it Sat. We're supposed to mail them by November fifteenth. Am leaving prices on things for duty. Will make out an approximate price list for customs also. Will send a check soon to cover this.

Could you send me some white yarn, Mom? I want a white ski cap, as we're all planning to go skiing in January. Mrs. Sohma said sh'd knit it for me. Also, she would like any bits of yarn to make slippers for the orphan children for Christmas. Could you send some extra for that? The poor kids have so little, & it's so cold in Karuizawa. Any color is okay, as she makes them variegated. She has Japanese girls help her knit for the orphans. According to the pattern, my cap will take six balls of white yarn.

Our room girl just brought Emilie & me each a huge bouquet of yellow & lavender chrysanthemums. They make the whole room smell so good.

Must close for tonight—my arms are a little swollen & sore & am very tired. All my love to my wonderful family.

Norma Jean

17 November 47

Dearest Folks,

It's Monday evening & decided to start the week out right by writing you. Received your grand letter this morning, Mom. Am always so glad to hear about the goings on at "310".

Am well & happy with life in Tokyo. Nothing too new has happened the past week. I mailed a package home November fifteenth. Don't open until December twenty-fifth. I included everyone's gift in it. Also stuck in a couple things without putting names on them. Either keep them or give them to our friends. It won't be much of a surprise as to the contents as I made out a customs declaration with prices, & put it on the outside. Also left prices on some of the things in case customs got snoopy. Sure hope it arrives on time. Will send a check next payday to cover customs tax.

The weather is crisp but clear. It is the chrysanthemum season now & they are beautiful. Since it is the Imperial flower, the Nips go all out for them.

It's hard for me to realize I've been away from home so long, but when you told me of Cathy Sue's talking, I realize how things must have been changing.

Larry really seems to be getting around—-must be the new car. Bet he sure can go for that home cooking. How are the meatless days for you? We haven't noticed any difference except we can't always get seconds on eggs for breakfast—which never bothered me if I got firsts or not.

Am enclosing a couple of pictures I just happened to see last night, as I was working on my photo album. The group picture was taken on the roof of the bank. I'm standing between the Major—the one I don't like--& Bessie the Korean auditor. The Japanese girls are typists in my section. Their names are Sumie-san & Matsisan. We've nicknamed them "Matty" & Suzy." They can't understand hardly any English & just giggle when you talk to them.

Goodnight dears.
Love,
Norma Jean

Thanksgiving Day, 1947

Dearest Mom, Dad, Esther, & Larry,

Today is Thanksgiving, & everyone is in such a gay mood, as the whole occupation is on a "holiday." Emilie & I have just finished breakfast. They were roasting the turkeys & the whole dining room smelled so good. Will enclose our menu—have to go down & copy it, as it's too long to remember. The waitresses are excited, & they're going to be all dressed up in kimonos this evening. I sent a telegram home yesterday. The telegraph office is right across from the Bank, so we all went over & sent messages home. It's a lovely day outside—just right for the football games.

The big event of the past week was the birthday party Lt. Kaity gave for his wife. They are the couple whose wedding I went to last spring. Everyone from our office was invited. I went with a Capt. who works there. It was really nice. We had a buffet supper, Hawaiian orchestra, & dancing. After she blew out the candles of the cake, the orchestra played "Happy Birthday." She & her husband danced together, & then the fellows cut in & danced with her, & we gals all danced with Lt. Kaity. The Col. was there & danced with each of us too. There were over a hundred people there. It was held in a beautiful room of the American Club.

Emilie & I are planning on taking a vacation in January & go skiing in the mountains. I can get skis from the hotel but need some ski pants, ski boots, & waterproof overmitts. Would you please buy these for me—will send you a check next payday. Emilie is asking for downhill style ski pants, as she likes them better. I don't particularly care—whichever you think is best. Don't spend too much—I don't need the very best. I will be able to use them quite a bit this winter & next I think. Will wear my sweaters & field jacket with them.

I was awfully sorry to hear you were sick, Mom. Take good care of yourself, dearie. Hope your taste is back for turkey today. Gad, I don't see how you work & keep the house up & entertain so much. I just work & everything else is done for me, & still I get so tired.

Must close for now. Hope you have a very, very happy Thanksgiving. Oh, yes, received Esther's darling card yesterday—it was so thoughtful.

Love to all,
Norma Jean

5 December 1947

Dearest Esther,

Received your swell letter today. Golly, what a lot of excitement! Also got letters & cards from Mom, Dad, & Larry today. It was the first mail I'd gotten in a week so really had a field day. Also got letters from Bobbie & Clarice. The mail boat was a little jammed they said. Sure did enjoy your pictures & clippings. Donna certainly looks like a lot of fun. Loved that "pot" pose of hers. The news of Lois & Archie's engagement really knocked me out. How I'd love to see your ring—sounds beautiful.

I never did call. I was sort of broke & didn't get paid until today, so couldn't call. Am very anxious to hear the details of your wedding plans. Is there anything special you'd like from this part of the world?

Have been at my usual mad pace. This last week was an endurance contest for me. This was my schedule.

Sat. Kabuki play—Went with some people who are missionaries here at a Jap. college.

Sun. Church in morning. Motor boating in Tokyo Bay in afternoon. Visiting Capt. Shephard from our office at the hospital in the evening.

Mon. Made arrangements for party next night.

Tues. Was official hostess for party at American Club for enlisted men at the office & their friends. I took my slide projector & they brought their slides. Served hor d'ouvers, drinks, nuts, cake & coffee. Had a guest list of thirty-five, & all but three came.

Wed. Bugaku at the Imperial Theatre. Will enclose program.

Thurs. Lt. & Mrs. Kaity had dinner with me here; then, we all went to the concert at the Imperial Theatre.

Fri. Here I am—dog tired, ready for a nice quiet weekend—I hope!

The funniest thing of the month was after the party Tuesday night. Emilie was going to eat dinner with me & go to the party too. She didn't come for dinner & didn't show up at the party. I couldn't figure it out, as she's usually so thoughtful about letting me know any change in her plans. I got home from the party at twelve o'clock. I could tell she hadn't come home from work yet, & I became worried. I called a fellow who we both know & who works in Emilie's section.

He had been at the party also & was wondering why Emilie wasn't there, as she told him she'd be there. We waited until 1 am, then, he came over to see what he could do. He decided we should look for her. We decided to check at the Provost Marshall's on accidents, etc.—he kept saying it would be so interesting to see what they do in the case of a missing person. We sat down there for an hour. They put the M.P.'s on "our case", & John & I kept calling places where we thought Emilie possibly could be. For about the tenth time, I called our hotel & Emilie answered. Golly, sure was glad to hear her voice. She had called me earlier but guess I was in the dining room. She said she sent a note to the American Club where the party was held, but I never got it. It seems she had an opportunity to meet some people who could help her with her plans for China so was with them all evening. The funny thing was when she went to work the next morning, the Provost Marshall's officers forget to tell all their agents that Emilie had been found. They called the Major who is E's supervisor, made him get up & go to the P.M. Office at 2:30 am to answer questions. The Major called some other girls at the offices, & they were all excited. Emilie walked into work fresh as a daisy, & all of these other people were haggard & tired from loss of sleep wondering where she was. We practically have hysterics about it now, but we sure were confused that night. Anyway, John & I now know what they do in case of a missing person, & Emilie knows the American Club doesn't deliver notes.

Am not going with the officer from the office anymore. We've been feuding all week. I got disgusted & gave him some things back that he gave me; he gave me some yen he owed me so we're all squared off. Just think we're both too independent & stubborn. Anyhow—it keeps life interesting.

Must close for tonight darling. Am so glad for your happiness. Think I will have to talk for a month steady to catch up when I get home. Goodnight for now,

Love,
Norma Jean

9 December 1947

Dearest Folks,

Am on my lunch hour at the Bank so will make this a quickie. Received the package mailed on Dec. 1st this morning. According to the sticker I'm to wait 'til Christmas so think I'll have Emilie hide it from me tonight—the temptation is too great.

I had a very nice birthday. Thank you so much for the cards & package. I loved the "knickknacks." Emilie gave me a gorgeous gold necklace & earring set. I also got some "Perhaps" perfume, corsage, & a bouquet of flowers. Capt. Shepherd of our office had a birthday Dec. 8th, so he remembered mine. I was awakened at 1:30 am Dec. 7th. He asked for "Miss Norma Jean Cone". When I answered, he sang "Happy Birthday" to me. I thought it was so cute of him. He said he wanted to be the first to congratulate me. He's in the hospital, so I went out & visited him on his birthday. Sunday morning, Emilie, Bessie, & Lois took me to church—said I should get a good start for my old age. In the afternoon, Emilie & I did our favorite Sunday afternoon diversion—riding buses around Tokyo. We just go across the street & pick out where we feel most like going. Most of the drivers know us now—if we had to pay they'd be making lots of money from us. In the evening saw "The Long Night".

Will enclose a forty-dollar money order for the customs tax & my snow clothes. Hope you have been able to buy them, as the other kids are all set for our January vacation. Tell me if this isn't enough money, & I'll send more.

Last Saturday, I met a stewardess from the American President Lines ship "Marine Adder". She was rather confused about getting around Tokyo by herself, so Emilie & I showed her some of the "outstanding" sights. She was very appreciative & bought us each some souvenirs. She's from L.A.—in the Crenshaw district--& took your name & address. She'll try to look you up when she returns. It may be some time, as she's going to Shanghai, Manila, & Honolulu before the States. Anyhoo—her name is Orena O'Neil. She's very interesting, as she's been a stewardess for years & has been all over.

Am at the Old Kaijo again. The mail clerk came in, so that settled my note writing. I got a beautiful red, wool, jersey blouse from Esther. It really fits & looks nice. Also got an interesting looking package from

Larry, which I'm saving. Kathryn Cullmer sent a darling birthday card & letter today, & I got my first Christmas card from June Blaine. Have just finished Scotch taping my cards on my sliding closet door.

Would you please send me some banana flakes & dried bananas? Emilie & I have been talking about bananas this evening & are drooling at this point. We're going to buy some PX ice cream & make banana sundaes. She's going to get syrup & coconut from Hawaii. Also need some more bobby pins—the PX never has them.

The officers at the Bank are planning a big party including a turkey dinner for all of us the day before Christmas. They won't tell me too much, but it sounds like fun.

I just re-read your last letter, Mom. I did get spanked on my birthday. As I was getting into bed Sat. night, I kicked one of the wooded slats out of the foot of my bed. The next day, Emilie picked it up & took advantage of my perfect spanking position.

I wanted to send David a Christmas card too but didn't know his address either. Tell him " Melly Clistmas" for me. Which reminds me of a sign we saw in a Japanese store today. It was painstakingly printed "Marry Xmas". Their spelling is just a riot. They just finished repainting safety signs all over town. The painter had put "Slow, Pefdestrans Crossing." There was one almost every corner.

Must close for now, as I'm itching to try the brass polish out on my candlesticks tonight. Goodnight & all my love,

Norma Jean

P.S. Am still awful glad I decided to come to your house December 7th.

P.S.#2 They're just beginning to get some rather nice tea sets in at the PX. Almost bought one last week but decided to wait to see if they'll get nicer ones soon.

15 Dec. 1947

Darling Esther,

It is Sunday evening & Emilie & I are spending a quiet evening reading & writing.

Thank you so much for the red jersey blouse—just love the style, & you know how I've always liked red! I opened it at the office & "the boys" have asked me every day since when I'm going to wear my sharp red blouse.

Sure enjoyed your last letter & snap shots.

Am mailing a package with this, which has some scarves & odds & ends in it. Hope they're okay. It's all they could offer at the PX now.

I imagine you're studying like mad for finals this weekend. Hope you come out well. At least, you won't have to go thru that ordeal again. Am sure anxious to hear your plans, kiddo.

I received the photographs of the folks for Christmas. I sure do like them—have been wanting their pictures. Will write them soon. Golly, they are so thoughtful & wonderful to me.

Am a bit stiff in the muscles tonight. It's the result of a rigorous night of barn dancing at the American Club last night. It was loads of fun. There were about 500 or 600 people there. Our group of eight was chosen as the best so we gave an exhibition of our barn-dancing techniques for every one. After that, they had a magician as part of the floorshow. I was enjoying his act when all at once he decided he needed a stooge. He asked me to come to the platform; my escort thought it was wonderful, so I stomped up to the stage. It was fun, as I always wondered what it would be like. He introduced me & asked if I had many friends in the audience. I said "quite a few". Then, he put a lemon, covered with a hanky, on my hand & asked if any of my friends would loan him some money—yen that is. Several offers were made. He chose one—read the serial number, then had me cut the lemon. I read the serial number from that, which was the same as the one from the audience. He said he had a present for me, but I would have to open it there. I was shrewd & opened it away from me—sure enough, a lot of papers flew out. When I got back to my seat, I told Ted I felt the American Club should pay us for entertainment, as we'd been in every act so far.

Ted is a very interesting person. He was a naval interpreter & speaks Japanese fluently. His father is a physicist in a university in India, & Ted also speaks one Hindu lingo. He's only 23 but a brain from way back. That's what makes it so interesting here—you meet the most unusual collection of people.

I bought a pair of opera glasses today at the PX. They're pretty nice & in a good leather case $3.90. They'll be perfect for traveling.

We had the best turkey dinner tonight. We always have an orchestra on Sunday evenings in our dining room.

Must close for tonight & get ready for another week's work. Have my hair washed but not curled yet. Thanks again for the wonderful birthday blouse.

All my love,
Norma Jean

16 Dec. 1947

Dearest Mom & Dad,

Received your most wonderful 7th of December letters today. Also received a swell one from Larry. You all sounded so happy that I felt especially happy today. You can't imagine what it means to have such a wonderful family! I really feel sorry for many of these 17 & 18 year old G.I.'s whose parents obviously neglect them.

Boy, am I anxious to get my ski clothes. I was so thrilled to hear you had gotten some. It sounds as though you did a perfect shopping job, Mom.

I bet you're all busy with plans for Esther & Dave. I'm so very glad its working out so well. Sure would like to see her ring. I like the date they set in February.

That would be awfully nice if Aunt Mary, Ida & Jonathan could come to California. Be sure & give them my best wishes. I often think about the wonderful time Esther & I spent in Kansas.

They're planning a big Christmas party for us at the bank. We'll get off at 11:30 on the 24th. All the officers are getting together & giving a big dinner & party. It will be right in our office—it is a beautiful room. The last I heard we're having turkey, ham, salads, & everything that goes with it. The Col. has ordered eggnog made. They're also inviting eleven of the big wheels of the Japanese Bank to be our guests.

Larry sounds so happy, & I'm so proud of his doing so well at work. He told me of his prospective new job—sounds very good.

Golly, most important part of this letter! I received your photographs. Am really proud of them, & you couldn't have given me anything I would enjoy more. Thanks loads & loads.

Merry Christmas to Mom, Dad, Esther & Larry.

Love,

Norma Jean

P.S. Emilie loved the Christmas card you sent her—that was so thoughtful. I sure liked the 'Cone' one. I showed it to everyone at work today, & they all got a big kick out of it. Esther, you can get one with "Bells" next year. Guess I'll have to marry someone with a Christmasy name too. Emilie's mother sent us big boxes of holly, & they came thru perfectly. She also sent us a box of Christmas goodies—candy, cakes, etc.

We're going to have a little party for our maids with the food box. The poor little girls work like beavers for us & always do little "extras." Don't even hang up my own clothes now.

Wed. Morning at Work—

Hurrah! It's snowing this morning. Lois & I threw snowballs at each other on the way to work & made a snowman in front of the Bank—more fun!

20 Dec. 1947

Dearest Folks,

Just a brief note tonight, as it's rather late. Emilie & I went to the Ernie Pyle Theatre & saw a Christmas program by the occupation school children & the show "Variety Girl." The kids were so cute.

My eyes have been so tired, & I had headaches quite often during this last week, so today, I took the afternoon off & went to the eye clinic. They gave me a good eye examination & said my eyes had changed since my glasses were fitted. Am enclosing the prescription they made & a money order. Will you please have some glasses made for me & sent airmail? I would like flesh color shell-rimmed ones. I don't want perfectly round ones but anything not extreme that you think would look okay on me. Don't know how much they'll cost but hope the M.O. will cover it.

Received your good letters & the gorgeous white yarn. Am planning on knitting right away.

Tomorrow afternoon, we're invited to Mrs. Sohma's Tokyo home for tea. Sunday we're going to hear the "Messiah" at Hibuja (sp?) Hall.

Am so sleepy. I just can't think anymore tonight. Will close for now. More soon.

Love,
Norma Jean

(Over)
Am making M.O. in Dad's name as I thought he might be more available for P.O. hours.

30 December 1947

Dearest Folks,

Golly, so much has happened since I last wrote you that I hardly know where to begin.

I had such a nice Christmas. Thank you so much for everything. The towels & soap were certainly welcome & nice. I gave Emilie one tube of shampoo, as we both like it very much. Esther, that subscription to the "Californian" was a wonderful idea—I sure like that magazine. Will write to Frances real soon—that blouse is sure pretty, & the yarn was wonderful. Larry sent me an awfully nice box of Tabu soap. I also got a pair of black Nylon stockings, brocade wallet, nightgown, bracelet, china condiment set, compact, & traveling toothbrush set. Aunt Frances & Grandma sent an awfully pretty blue towel washcloth with "Yankee Clover" soap. The day before Christmas, we had a party at the office. There were about 50 there. We had a buffet luncheon. They took movie pictures, & I am going to see the results tonight. Christmas Eve, Emilie & I went to services at a missionary church. Two fellows & we were the only Americans there. Later, we went to a dance. Christmas Day, we visited a Japanese family in Kamakura. It was a cold but nice day. Gee, is it ever cold now. I just freeze at work—no heat in Japanese buildings. We only have three little electric heaters in our large office. This weekend, Emilie & I went to Nikko. It takes about 5 hours on the train & is northwest of Tokyo. We stayed in a Japanese Hotel & ate in an Allied Hotel. It's a very famous resort in Japan & is famous for its shrines.

Received your swell letter today, Esther. Golly, what wonderful wedding plans! Sure am keeping my fingers crossed that you'll get the apartment. I love the colors you've chosen for your attendants. To be very frank, I do get a little homesick when I think of not seeing your wedding but just can't be two places at once, darn it!

I've gotten so many lovely Christmas cards & letters this year. Mrs. Wallis of Spokane wrote the nicest letter, which I plan to answer soon. Am making my usual New Year's resolution—write more letters.

Some of the G.I.'s from our office have left for the States. I gave them your address in case they come through California. They are all pretty young—probably will go right home from the port. Best you don't say much about my going with any of the officers at the bank— scuttlebutt gets back awfully fast, & I don't like to have a discriminatory feeling among the enlisted men—little do they know. Probably one or two will make the southbound trip. Mom, if Johnny Spadecia comes be sure & tell him about our vacation in the San Bernardino Mts. I was telling him about it one afternoon, & he kidded me for weeks about "hot rocks." He said he'd like to hear it from you—think he didn't believe me. He was always so nice to me at work.

It's time to go see the Christmas movie—they're waiting for me downstairs.

Bye now—

Love,
Norma Jean

Eleven

Dear Frances,

What a wonderful Christmas present I received from "312"! I was so surprised & really thrilled with the blouse. The handwork is gorgeous, & I love the style. Sure will be proud to wear it. I've tried it on several times, & it fits perfectly. Thank you so much. Also, want to thank you for the yarn. Mrs. Sohma was thrilled with it. She especially liked the variety of colors. They knit slippers for Japanese war orphans with it. They will certainly be appreciated as it's so cold here now, & the children have nothing but the wooden sandals.

There seems to be a lot of excitement at "310" now with Esther's wedding plans. Remember the details, Frances, as I've got to hear all about it when I get home, & they may forget something in the excitement.

Today is New Years, & the Japanese are all agog with the holiday spirit. For the first time, all the maids have the day off. All the natives have learned to say Happy New Year in English, which, in many cases, is their whole English vocabulary beside "Okay". One of the waitresses got a bit excited this morning & said "A New Happy Year."

We took a ride this morning, & everyone looked so nice in their colorful kimonos. The children looked like little dolls. Lots of the little girls had white fur collars. The boys were out flying their kites, & the girls were playing with battledores (something like badminton).

The Imperial Palace grounds are open today for the Japanese, & we have been watching the throngs going in from our windows. We are having a big New Years dinner this evening at the Hotel. They have our dining room all decorated. Someone decided that big pictures of babies should be the motif. We all about died laughing when we saw these huge pictures all over the walls. The artist wasn't too shrewd at proportions, & the poor things look like abnormalities from a medical journal.

Have had a very nice holiday season but can't help be glad it's over. Everyone has that party-weary look at this point. We had a day & a half off for Christmas & New Years. Emilie & I are as busy as usual with school, meetings, dates, & sight seeing. We're all set for our skiing vacation in three weeks. Finally located an Allied Hotel where we could get reservations. All of them near Tokyo are filled with dependants who are waiting for their houses to be finished. We are going to Kanazawa, which is about a 19 hour train ride southwest of Tokyo. Have been saving those yellow mittens & yellow sweater you sent for the occasion.

Certainly miss our maid service today. Emilie has her half of the room all straightened up, so best at this point I get started on my half.

Thank you again for your lovely Christmas card, blouse, & yarn. I certainly appreciate your thoughtfulness. Give my regards to everyone & a "New Happy Year" to you all.

Love,
Norma Jean

8 Jan 1948

Dearest Folks,

Have just washed my hair, worked the daily crossword puzzle & am listening to some good radio music.

Received the ski clothes & my glasses today. Golly, the clothes are swell. Am wearing the socks now. The pants are large, but Emilie said they're supposed to be like that so other clothes will fit beneath.

Can hardly wait for our vacation now. We were going Jan. 19th, but the Major wouldn't let me off then, so we're going Feb. 9th instead. We have our reservations at the Asokanko Hotel. It's on the southern island of Kyushu & is on the active volcano, Mt. Aso.

I sure like the style you chose for my glasses—just what I wanted. I don't know where I stand financially, as there was no bill with the glasses. Let me know if I owe you more. We have to pay our income tax before next June 15 so am trying to save $300 now, so I can pay it by March or April. They just started this month to deduct income tax from our checks.

Sure did enjoy my phone visit with you. It was so good to hear your voices again. Was terribly sorry to hear of Esther's & Dad's illness. I got your letter, mom, telling of your Christmas & Lois' visit. Those customs men make me <u>so</u> mad—it's discouraging. I don't see how those silver mugs could ever get bent the way I originally packed them. I meant the box of masks for Dave—sure laughed when I heard his name was on the apron. Your bracelet & earrings are Damascene, Mom. If you ever see them in the states would like to know how much they price them there. Did they charge any customs on the scarves?

Esther, I've been wondering about the bond situation & your coming change of name. Would you want me to change the name on the bonds or maybe send you cash instead? You know how slow this Army is; I thought best I'd better ask you now.

Nothing too new in Tokyo. The Nips are still celebrating New Years. Monday, I saw a whole bunch of men walking down the Ginza. They were dressed all alike in red & blue "Happy" coats. They were shouting, singing, & moaning weird sounding things & waving big banners. I asked the Japs at the office who they were. They thought about it for three days, then finally figured out they were the firemen welcoming the New Year.

Must close for tonight. Have to put up my hair & fix my nails yet.

Love,
Norma Jean

17 Jan 1948

Darling Esther,

What a wonderful sister you are! Emilie & I received our blouses in yesterday's mail & are just crazy about them. Emilie just loves those frilly clothes, & she looks so nice in them too. She wore hers last night on her date. Our imaginations went into action & today we're making cotton slips trimmed in eyelet lace that I had gotten at the PX last summer. She had already sent for a "new look" skirt pattern & we're each going to make black skirts for our blouses. Golly, those are the cutest blouses & they fit both of us perfectly. Emilie has the blue & I the green & grey stripe. Thanks a million, Esther. It was so nice of you to remember Emilie too. Her mother sent me some black nylons for Christmas—which I can wear with my new Gibson girl outfit.

It's a beautiful morning & since it's Saturday have been gadding about Tokyo. Several Army units have been drilling & marching past the Hotel, so have been busy as a beaver all morning.

I got a raise at work. My annual salary is now $2992. Sure can use it now for my last year's income tax. I was a CAF-2 when I came; now I'm a CAF-4. Emilie is a CAF-4 too.

Tonight, am going to the British Theatre "Piccadilly" to see Nicholas Nicolby. They show only British films there, & it's free to all Allied personnel. There are always more Americans there than anyone else. Our movies cost 30¢, & since you have to pay in American scrip very few Allies can go.

Must close as Emilie is home now, & we want to get started on our slips. Thanks again for the darling blouses.

All my love,
Norma Jean

27 Jan 1948

Dearest Mom, Dad, Esther & Larry,

Just got home from work & decided to at least start a letter to "you all" before my dinner guest comes.

It's been a beautiful day. It rained yesterday, but the sun shone so brightly all day today that everyone felt as though spring had come. The cold weather is expected to start any time now. February is usually about their coldest month.

Have been very busy gadding about. Last Wednesday, Emilie, Bessie & I went to the War Crimes Trial. They give us time off to see them, as we're all urged to go. We got press tickets so sat in the press section. We saw everything very well. We had earphones over which you could hear everything they said & could turn the switch for Japanese, English, French or Russian translation. The day we were there, they were trying Oshima, the Japanese Ambassador to Germany. All twenty-four Japanese defendants were there, including Tojo & Togo. They just looked like another straggly bunch of Nijas—all looked quite bored with everything. There are eleven judges from the various Allied nations. Sir William Webb from Australia presides, & if any question comes up, he confers with the others. He really gives the prosecution & defense a bad time, as he's so sarcastic.

29 Jan 1948

As you see I didn't get far with that letter.

I received the invitation to Esther's wedding today. It made it seem so official. I like the invitation very much—it's already in my scrapbook with her news clippings.

Have been laughing all day about my last night's date so must tell you. A friend called & said some of our mutual British friends were leaving & wanted me to have dinner & see them off. One is going to Hong Kong with others to England. The three fellows & I had dinner at the British Empire house then took them to the train. After we left them we had a little trouble with the Jeep. We were about two blocks from the station when it stopped altogether. The fellows were looking in the engine, & I was holding matches. Soon some buddies of the Britishers came by & stopped to help. The Jap guards from the Hotel across the street saw us & brought flashlights. Just then the M.P.'s came by & saw I was holding lights & thought I might need help, so they stopped & helped. Soon we noticed more people around. It seemed that they saw M.P.'s, flashlights, & a crowd so thought there was an accident or something. Traffic became congested, & we had a huge audience telling them how to put the wires together. They finally fixed it, & the crowd went away. Ken lived in the Hotel across the street so said goodnight. Dave decided he had to keep the engine roaring 'cause he was afraid to have it stop. We turned around & were going past Ken's hotel (roaring like mad) when all of a sudden Ken pops out from two parked jeeps, pulls out a big white handkerchief & flags us off, just like at the races. I was knocking myself out laughing, & Dave was still as serious as a Totem pole as he was concentrating madly on keeping the engine roaring.

Have worn the blouse Esther sent me several times already & have gotten so many compliments on it.

Our meals are being raised from 25¢ to 40¢. The difference is just about my new raise. Lots are complaining but, good heavens, where else could you get three good meals for $1.20 a day?

Must close for tonight, as I want to finish my slip. All I have to do is put eyelet lace around one-half of the hem yet. I imagine you're all terribly busy now. Sure love to hear from you but will understand if you're too busy, as writing takes time, & you can write the details later at your leisure. Goodnight to all.

Love,
Norma Jean

2 Feb. 1948

Dearest Folks,

Received your wonderful letters, Esther & Mom. I really appreciate your telling me of your gifts & shower parties, Esther. Your friends surely are good to you & I'm so happy for you.

I sure enjoyed your newsy letter, Mom. When you mentioned the man at the State Department, I thot it was funny, because the State Dept. building is right across the street from the Bank of Japan, & they park their cars in our front parking lot. Am awful at looking people up, so doubt I'll ever locate the man.

I do want you to keep any money I had left over for postage, etc. I should give you a commission for all the running around you've done for me. The glasses fit—put them on immediately & haven't worn the old ones since.

Tuesday Evening—

Emilie came in last night & that stopped my—ya-ta-ta, ya-ta-ta. It snowed for about an hour this afternoon (was very cold all day). We were just freezing in our unheated office. The Col. then came in with a sparkle in his eye & said he'd gotten 350 tons of coal, & it was delivered this afternoon. None of us said another word about being cold. He'd gone to Headquarters in Yokohama & gone through lots of red tape & got the coal & an electricity allocation, so we can have the elevator running again. This is Col. Sprinkle, Col. Adams left for the states. Col. Sprinkle is better known among us as "the little drip"—he's really very nice.

Tomorrow night, we're going to see "The Mikado." Emilie saw it last night & said it was very good.

We're getting all set for our next week's vacation. Will take our ski clothes. Have bought booklets on Kyushu, snacks, & a pocketknife, so all I have to do now is organize things.

I finally bought some pearls. I stood in line from 12:30 'till 4:00 but I got them. They cost $16.10 & are now being strung & a clasp put on them. If they are good (sure look nice), they should be worth quite a bit in the States. When I get enough energy will go through it again for a strand for you, Mom. We're rationed one strand every 3 months. It was quite funny as we all became chummy in line, & I went

& got popcorn & others got cokes, & we all brought reading material to pass our line-standing time.

Must close for tonight & start organizing.

All My Love
XXXX OOOOO
Norma Jean

12 Feb. 1948

Dearest Folks,

Am in the midst of my vacation & am truly having a glorious time. Will give you my itinerary thus far & finish it on the train home.

Friday, Feb. 6—Left Tokyo at 7:40 p.m. Emilie started the next day, as her travel authority hadn't come through. I had already bought my ticket & checked my bags so decided to wait at Kyoto & meet her on the train from there. I had a compartment & had a nice trip.

Saturday—Arrived at Kyoto 5:50 a.m. In the morning, I took a sightseeing tour of Buddhist temples & Shinto shrines. Very interesting—had good guides who explained everything. The Buddhist temples were cold, & we had to take our shoes off to go through—hmm! At one, the Buddhist Priestesses shaved their heads. Next, I had to find a place to stay, as I had no time to make reservations. I got completely snarled up in Army red tape—you just don't go places without direct orders & reservations here. Capt. Vickerman & his wife had previously invited me to visit them here, so I called them. They came right over in their car (I ate at the Kyoto hotel with no difficulty). As they only have a one-room apartment, they decided I should stay at the hotel. Col. Devin, who was also previously from the Bank, is the Commanding Officer for Military Gov't in this region. Capt. V. called him, & he immediately told the major in charge to let me in at the hotel. He wanted to see me & invited us to his hotel. We all had an old home week about the Bank. He wrote a letter for me right then, which may help in getting a better paying job. (It sure helps to know the right people I'm beginning to think.) In the afternoon, Capt. & Mrs. V. took me all around Kyoto & to the best shopping districts. Kyoto is about the most famous tourist city, as there is so much to see, & it is typical of pre-war Japan, as it was not bombed.

Sunday—Got up at 4:30 a.m. in order to make the train Emilie would be on. Got to the station & had an awful time buying another ticket because of my travel orders not including Kyoto. Finally got it settled, dashed out to track four, only to find the train slowly pulling out. Emilie had gotten up to see me on—it was the funniest feeling. I just stood at the track & watched her go away. Since I was still in Kyoto, decided to take the day tour to Nara—another famous spot. Sooo—I went back & got the 9 o'clock sightseeing bus. It was a beautiful trip. It took an hour & a half from Kyoto. We visited more temples, shrines & saw a deer park (lots of tame deer roaming around). Returned to Kyoto at 4 p.m. & got the 7:48 train out—no complications this time.

Monday—Lovely train ride. Rode along the beautiful inland sea & had luscious meals. Went through Hiroshima & Kobe. After three train changes & a bus ride arrived at the Aso Kanko Hotel at 7:30 p.m. Emilie was in the lobby, & we laughed & laughed about our missing trains. After dinner, played Bingo & retired early. This is the nicest hotel I've been in yet. Lovely tile bathroom, wonderful beds, & luscious meals. They also have a natural hot sulfur pool.

Tuesday—At 9 a.m. left for Tachinochi (1 & 1/2 hours) for swimming & a steak fry. The weather was beautiful, very bright sunshine. The swimming pool had natural hot mineral water & the steaks were wonderful. Japanese boys & a G.I. did all of the cooking, cleaning up, etc. The place is located at the foot of a tiny valley over whose cliffs four waterfalls flow. It's terrific! In the evening saw Kendo exhibition (something like dancing with bamboo swords).

Wednesday—Took sightseeing tour to Kumamoto. Visited an antique shop where I bought a goofy tea set. Next, we went to the ancient Kumamoto Castle then had lunch at the Red Cross Hilltop Club. As we were all coming out, an old lady asked if we wanted our fortunes told. We all did & have been comparing & laughing about our futures every since. Went to the Camp Wood PX & snack bar, railroad station for return reservations, more shopping then home. It was a 1 & 1/2 hour trip each way over awfully bumpy roads. It had snowed the night before but was a bright sunny day, which made the mountain views breathtakingly beautiful. In the evening saw "Golden Earrings" at Hotel.

Thursday—Played tennis all morning with Navy Officer. In the afternoon, hiked to summit of mountain. Beautiful view, but oh my aching legs! We had to hike through lots of snow & mud, but with the sun beating down, didn't get a bit cold. We have beautiful sunburned faces now. In the evening, saw Judo exhibition by members of the Kumamoto police force.

Friday—In the morning four of us went horseback riding. Never have I seen such stubborn horses! Mine wouldn't go through any mud holes, so we didn't get far on the bridle paths. We just walked down the road. Even old "Blue" at Barton Flats would have outdistanced this one. The others were as bad as mine, so we all gave up after an hour.

In the afternoon, we got on the bus for Mt. Aso. It was 27 miles & took nearly two hours. We walked for about 20 minutes to reach the summit. They weren't kidding when they said this was an active volcano. It sounded like tremendous thunder, & smoke & steam came out in clouds. All of a sudden, it would stop for 20 seconds. This deathly silence was rather frightening at first. It was so active & hot that afternoon we couldn't get to the nearest edge but stayed on one above it. This is one of the volcanoes where many Japanese lovers have committed suicide. It was cold & started to rain. We hiked back to the hotel, & it only took us 40 minutes, as the hotel is directly below. It was certainly easier than riding a bus over bumpy roads for two hours. The last eruption of Aso was May 1947—you probably read about it last year. Coming down was fun—the trails were just mud about 8 inches deep. They were slippery too with all the lava content. We all fell several times & looked like mud pies by the time we strolled into the hotel.

In the evening, we saw the movie "California," packed our suitcases & said farewell to the lucky ones staying on.

Saturday-Four of us left at 6:30 a.m. They were Barbara (a nurse), "Doc," a Lt., Emilie & me. At one o'clock we arrived at Fukuoka, & since we had a three-hour layover, "Doc" invited us to eat at the 128th Hospital Officers Club. We had a lovely lunch & climbed back onto the four o'clock train. We got to the Inland Sea just as the sun was setting.

Sunday—What a gorgeous, bright, sunny, day. The farmers were all out, & the snow-capped mountains in the distance were like a background painting. We played cribbage, etc., & talked mostly about what we'd like to eat. We passed Fuji just as the sun was setting behind it--the perfect way to end a Japanese vacation.

It's Monday & we've gotten into the usual week's routine. Received the best things in the mail when I got home. Esther, that was so thoughtful to send Emilie & me the package & cards—we sure love them. Am planning on taking them on our skiing trip next weekend. Sure have thought about you this weekend. I figured out that you would be getting married on Sunday our time. Saturday night, we made a toast to you, & Sunday, I kept saying "my Sister's almost married now." After awhile, if I hadn't mentioned it, "Doc" would ask me about it, & we would all talk about "Esther & Dave" again. They were all swell people & lots of fun. I sure liked your letters. Am getting some stamps tomorrow & will send them this week.

A Sgt. from the Bank is going home & will either call you up or see you, if he possibly can. His name is Max Cornell & he is really a very nice person. He has wonderful color slides of Japan. If he has time he would show them to you if you could get a projector. Do try, if he comes, as his pictures are really good. He showed them at a party I gave for the Enlisted Men & also at our mutual Japanese friend's home. He's had some college & is registered for the fall term in Michigan I believe. He is also interested in our LARA group, so we became good friends. He's a strict Christian Scientist & was really an outstanding enlisted man. I sure hope you can meet him. Larry, I also gave him your address in case he stops in Bakersfield; I know you'd like him a lot. Oh, Yes, Larry am sending some scarves. Didn't have much choice but will send these now & more later if they get some cute ones.

Will you please send this to Larry. Must close for tonight—you must have eyestrain at this point of my scribbling. Goodnight & all my love to Mom, Dad, Esther, Dave, & Larry.

Norma Jean

24 Feb. 1948

Dearest Family,

It is Tuesday morning & am again in the midst of unpacking suitcases & getting things in shape after an out-of-town weekend.

Friday night, Emilie, John & I left on the ten p.m. train for Sugadairaguchi for skiing. We sat up all night, but all slept most of the time. At four thirty a.m. they awakened us, & we got off at Ueda, which is northwest of Tokyo. It is in the mountains & was very cold. We climbed into a funny Japanese bus & rode up into the mountains over bumpy roads for an hour. At the end of the bus line, we got off. A horse & sleigh was supposed to take us three miles further to our hotel, but as the roads were nothing but ice we couldn't ride, so walked. Gad, what a walk! Three miles <u>up</u> slippery trails—we'd take one step & slide back two. It was gorgeous country & the sun was just coming up. There was lots of snow, & the trees, creeks, etc. looked so beautiful. About 2 & 1/2 hours later, we arrived. They met us with hot cups of tea & a good wood fire. We were just famished so ate our "K" rations & huge bowls of rice. It was a nice Japanese Hotel but as usual no heat in the rooms. We had "kutatsu" (charcoal burner in the floor with blankets over it under which you keep your hands & feet warm while your back freezes). We slept in the morning & went skiing all afternoon. The slopes were wonderful for beginners, & the hotel manager gave us all skiing lessons. Sunday was gorgeous. The snow was piled up all around, & the sun shone brightly. They were getting ready for a local ski meet, & you could hear the ski songs all over the valley on the loud speaker. It was worth the struggle of getting there, we thought then! We were skiing all day & came in with good suntans.

We were the only Americans in the hotel, but there was a ski club nearby. The members were mostly British, but there were also some Americans, a Frenchman, a Turk, & Australians. We visited their lodge, & they paid us a very formal call at our hotel. John speaks Japanese very well & was wonderful in helping us with everything. He really knows Japan & the Japanese. Monday morning we got up early. Outside it was snowing heavily & blowing a gale. This time it was too cold to ride the sleigh so we had to ski down to the bus. We surely didn't get cold plowing through the snow. I got almost to the bottom when my ski strap broke, so I rode the sleigh for about the last 1/2 mile. We arrived in Tokyo at 10 o'clock last night. I thought I'd be tired & stiff today, but golly, I've never felt more full of pep. Emilie & I both noticed our added vitality—guess the fresh air & exercise was what we needed.

Thought I'd get lots of mail today, but the mail clerk brought none. The distributors had a holiday, so no one had any. Am anxious to hear of the wedding events.

Golly, sure am glad for my ski clothes. Emilie & I are planning one more ski trip before the season closes. Gee, am having such a good time! Seems like one long vacation.

Goodnight to my wonderful family.

All my love always,
Norma Jean

Twelve

Dearest Family,

This is the first evening I've been home this week (& the only one for the rest of the week). So much has been going on. I was so anxious to hear from you about the wedding. I received Esther's & Dave's lovely letter from Catalina last Saturday & Mom's yesterday. Golly, the wedding sounded out-of-this world. The gifts are surely lovely & such a wonderful selection. I read to Emilie about her gift as her mother got it for her in Seattle. She's been nearly as enthused about it all as I have been. Now we're waiting for the pictures. The write-up & picture in the paper was very nice—it's already in my scrapbook of important events.

Last Monday night was a very interesting experience for Emile & me. A mutual friend of ours, Ted Otteson, is going home, & we were invited to a farewell party for him by a fellow in the diplomatic section of the State Department. Our invitations were very formal & were delivered to our offices by a G.I. from the S.D. We "formally" accepted. It was formal dress; Emile wore a black evening skirt with black evening sweater, which had gold sequins. I wore my black evening skirt & pink evening blouse with sequins that Esther had sent. Ted picked us up at 7:15. The host, Mr. Burnett, lives in the loveliest home with about three other S.D. foreign diplomatic officers. Have never seen such a perfect host in all my life. There were about 20 there. First, we all had "Old Fashion" cocktails & hors d'oeurvres. We all were given slips with a name of a famous couple on it—our dinner partner was the other name of the couple. Dinner was buffet style & was wonderful—turkey, rare roast beef, salads, relishes, potatoes, vegetables & lots of very fancy dishes. With this we had white wine. For dessert we had cherry tarts with whipped cream. Later, in another room they served demitasse & brandy. We girls took an interest in the house, so the host gave us a tour—what a dream place. Most of the people there could speak about three languages & several sang songs in German, Russian, Japanese, & French. It all seemed so international & fascinating. They had scads of maids in pretty kimonos. Just before it broke up, we had champagne & toasts to Ted. He is going to the States, then to India where his father is a physics teacher at a university. He lived there most of his childhood.

The whole occupation is in an uproar. The Army is settling back to a peacetime organization & its new career plan. All officers who are over age for their rank, or who were not a Sergeant in 1941 have to be back in the States by June. We're losing all but the Col., Major & one Lt. Boy, it's killing most of them. They admit they've been on a gravy train for 7 or 8 years now. They're starting to send them next month. They can go back to the rank of Master Sgt. but most can't stand the thought of it. They also hate to think of competing in civilian life again. Lots are trying to get jobs here & stay in Japan on Civil Service. That's all I hear at work now—these decisions are driving them insane.

We think we're going skiing this weekend, but our reservations are a little hazy. Will leave tomorrow night, if they go through.

John is here & is going to let us know about the reservations so must close & go down & settle things.

Love to all,
Norma Jean

8 March 1948

Dearest Folks,

It's Monday evening & am waiting for Emilie to come home from work. I just remembered that I had sent a box of stuff home a week or so ago & had forgotten to tell you about it. It's things I've collected, & as our space is so limited, decided to send them home. It's mostly junk but some of it was given to me, so I'll want it later. I mailed it fourth class so can't tell how long it will take. Tell me how much the duty is, & I'll pay you.

List of package
Two Brass candlesticks—(from the dump). I left them in the rough more or less so customs could tell they were old—shouldn't be any duty.
Cherrywood cigarette box—I like the wood in it.
Wooden puzzle box—anyone who wants to be puzzled can have this—I taped directions on the outside.
Coins—I have some more here if anyone wants those.
China windbell
Clay charms
China Buddha's—Mrs. O'Neill gave them to me. They are Satsuma china. One pair Chopstick holders.

I ran out of stationery, & this was all I could find--from Kenmore Hall. New York seems like a dream to me now. The East was fun but hope I never have to make my home there.

We didn't go skiing this weekend. We were going to a Japanese Hotel but couldn't find out for sure if it had been put "On Limits", so decided against it. If we are arrested by the M. P.'s for anything we get a D.R. (Delinquency Report). If you get three, they send you home—forces you into being good if you want to stay. You can get them for lots of things—even for leaving a paper marked "Secret" unlocked at work. I'm in charge of checking on this every evening at work now.

We are on a limited water ration starting now. It's been so dry this year that the water level is expected to reach the critical point Wednesday. On Wednesday, we'll be on an emergency ration. Guess we're just trying to keep up with California.

Emilie came in so must close & go down & eat dinner.

All my love,
Norma Jean

11 March 1948

Dearest Esther & Dave,

Am waiting for Emilie to come home from work again. Golly, this week has gone so quickly & I've done nothing particularly exciting. Received your note today, Mrs. Bell. Your stationery is very nice. I can imagine what a job your thank-you's were. The reception napkins were just darling.

The biggest excitement of the Occupation this week is MacArthur's decision of "not refusing" if the American people choose him to run for president. I was walking back to work Tuesday when I saw a little Japanese man running down the street ringing a bell & selling papers like mad. I asked a Japanese man who could speak English what all the excitement was, & he said "MacArthur to be American President." All the Nips were excited, & we think very optimistic about Mac's election possibilities. The Occupation took it with tongue-in-cheek. There is hardly any American political talk here.

The water rationing went into effect Wednesday. We're scarcely affected as all the large Allied billets & offices are supplied. In smaller replacements & for the natives, water is available only a few hours a day. Sure do hope it rains soon.

The civilian girl who works for me, Lois, at the Bank is getting married next month. She was going to have a large wedding, & I was going to be a bridesmaid, but it's so hard to get things, she's decided on a very small wedding. Ten of us are going to be their witnesses & then have a wedding party at the American Club. I've been helping her with her trousseau, & it's really a two-man job here. She's having things made, as she's so small, she can't order things & have them fit well. She's marrying a Sergeant who is awfully nice.

Sure hope you get a home of your own soon, as I know it will be so thrilling to use all of your lovely wedding presents. It's time for Emilie to be here so must close.

All my love to my

Favorite "Mr. & Mrs."
Norma Jean

21 March 1948

Dearest Mamasan & Papasan,

It's Sunday evening, & Emilie & I have been washing our hair, polishing our nails & getting ready for another week's work. I have been terribly busy at work lately & need a running start on it for the week. The auditors took several months to audit our work, & now an Army board of a Lt Col., Major, Capt., & Lt. are here for two months to check the discrepancies found by the auditors. Since it was published in the last week, I can tell you about one phase we've been working on like mad. It's the Revolving Fund being set up to aid in Japan's economic rehabilitation[25]. You may have read about it, eh? It's interesting but the accuracy of all the figures due to international politics make it very tedious work. If you hear from me in Sugamo prison it will probably be due to a proofreading mistake. Rough occupation!

One of the officers brought his radio last week, & we all listened to President Truman's speech at 2:30.[26] Golly, things are so unsettled all over the world. We're all kidding about meeting in the Russian Occupation or Siberia's salt mines.

It's been raining off & on all week. This has helped the water shortage. The Japanese are rationed to water for just two hours a day. They will be rationed like this until June at least, the papers say, as the water level is so low they are not going to allow more water used until a reserve is built up. They have to boil or disinfect all the water as it's contaminated from the low-level reservoirs. We haven't been affected but are asked to conserve.

I hadn't been to a show for quite a while then saw three in three days. I saw "The Best Years of Our Lives," "The Fugitive," & "The Lady from Shanghai".

Yesterday at the PX, I bought a very nice, all metal, footlocker for $12.65. You sure collect a lot of things—hate to think of the packing job ahead.

---

25 Essentially, the "Revolving Fund" was designed to permit Japan to borrow up to $150,000,000 against the assets of the Bank of Japan: gold, silver, & jewelry. The international lenders included the U.S. Import-Export Bank. The objective was to allow Japan to import raw materials, particularly cotton.

26 This probably refers to the March 12, 1948 speech of President Truman to the Congress in which essentially there was a declaration of actively containing Communism.

Have Esther & David gotten a home yet? I get so excited when I think of visiting them & seeing all of their presents. Emilie & I have just been figuring out—she's been here in Tokyo two years next week & hasn't been home in 3 & 1/2 years as she came here from Hawaii. She only had a nine-month contract in Japan but hasn't wanted to leave yet. Lots of the kids are ready to stay for the duration of the occupation. They go home for 20 or 45 days a year on vacation & are happy to come back to Tokyo. They admit "they've never had it so good". What a crazy life. Must close for tonight.

Love,
Norma Jean

26 March 1948

Dearest Dad,

Happy Birthday, Father!!! Will be thinking of you especially hard on the 7th of April & wishing you the happiest of birthdays.

Received your wonderful package yesterday. The candy was super—the first chocolate covered cherries I've had since I left America, & jeepers, did they ever taste good. They came through very well & tasted so fresh. I liked & needed the bobby pins & hairpins, too. Now I have enough calendars for my room & office both. Thank you so much for everything.

It doesn't seem like it can be Easter time already. The rain has stopped, & it was a gorgeous day today so we did get the springtime feeling. The cherry trees are starting to bud around Tokyo now, & the most beautiful time in Japan is almost here. Emilie & I have reservations at Kyoto next month at the peak of the season. The cherry blossoms & wisteria are supposed to be the most beautiful there. We'll go down just for the weekend.

Last night, I went to an Easter Cantata at a Finnish Missionary church. John played the organ & had charge of the music, & I was the only other American there. Everyone in the church (about 20) was in the choir & three Japanese, the Finnish missionary & his wife & myself were the audience. The music was very good—a Bach number--& the singers were excellent as most were students & some graduates of music conservatories.

Everyone was allowed time off today, Good Friday, for church if they wanted. My supervisor, a Lt., said he was going & asked me what church I went to. He is Catholic & said he thought I might be. I was kidding him & told him "Four-Square Gospel"; then a G.I. came along & said "Jean & I are Baptists & are going to the Protestant Services." Being a gorgeous day, everyone kidded us about shopping on the Ginza instead of going to church. The Lt. went to his service, & at three (as we were told by Special Services), we went to ours. We got in the Chapel & noticed something was wrong. We just about died when we realized we were at the Catholic service. The Lt. had said he was going to check on us as we left, & every time we thot of him seeing us "good Baptists" at a Catholic service, we practically rolled under the kneeling boards. The G.I. decided we should string along. We were up & down, up & down for 45 minutes. When we tried to walk down the chapel stairs at the end our knees felt so wobbly that we staggered. We were laughing all the way back. The first question the Lt. asked us when he saw our merry faces was "What was the sermon about?" Ah, but we had our proof—our knees were dirty! He really got a charge out of it.

I got the best letters from Mom & Esther today & the grand snapshots of Esther & Dave at Catalina.

So you've sold the Chev! Bet Jim has a hard time keeping it from turning in at 310. You will have room for lots of "good old stuff" in the garage now. Gad, it might be hard to realize it's home without the old landmark.

Am very busy helping Lois get ready for her wedding. Another girl & I are giving her a shower April first, & tomorrow I'm going to comb Tokyo for decorations, shower gifts, prizes & a wedding gift. Our office got them a beautiful cutwork linen tablecloth & 8 napkins for $25.00 at the PX.

Well, Pop, take good care of yourself. I want you to be in good form if I ever decide to take the walk down the aisle—it'd probably be a race.

'By for now & all my love,
Norma Jean

29 March 1948

Dearest Folks,

Just got home from work. We were so busy that the wheels of production seem to be still turning in my head. They hired a new girl today & she will begin tomorrow—another typist for me to keep busy. My "crew" now includes three American civilians, three Japs & one G.I. Just wish my pay would increase with the personnel.

I had a very nice Easter. We went down to Enoshima & Chikasaki in a Jeep. It was a gorgeous day, & the ocean was so pretty. Emilie & I got all dressed up for Easter breakfast & were going to church but were late by the time breakfast was over, so didn't make church.

In your last letter, you asked about the clothes situation. Mom, I need a bag desperately. I want a black, over-the-shoulder one for traveling. Also am at the critical shoe stage. I need some dressy, black flats & some dressy heels (sandals I think, any color). I need a new date dress very badly—ugh, this clothes problem. We can't quite figure what's in style in the States by the rumors we hear. The magazine styles don't look too drastic to me. Anyway, I'd like a sharp looking dress for spring, if you see one. My finances are in their usual confusion. I have to have $280 by June for income tax, which I have to save yet. We're so far behind our payroll that when we do get paid I usually have it already spent. I will send some money the next pay, but could you send the shoes & bag as soon as you get a chance?

I surely did like your wedding letter, Mom. Am curious about the Bakersfield property deal, anything new?

This is an awful shortie, but I have to make decorations like mad tonight for Lois' shower. More later.

All my love,
Norma Jean

Thirteen

5 April 1948

Dear Folks,

It's Sunday afternoon & have had a nice lazy day. The sun shone so brightly all day that two other girls & I have been sun bathing on the roof most of the day. Emilie is working until 9 tonight, & we three gals decided to go see "Green Dolphin Street" later after dinner.

I got that wonderful box of snacks & wedding cake. It all tasted so good. When we came in this afternoon, I opened the potatoes, & they were luscious with cold cokes. The dried fruit is marvelous, as our meals & PX snacks do get a little monotonous. The cake must have been gorgeous. I ate most of mine &, of course, dreamed on the rest. It was a little dry, but the icing was very good.

The day I got the package I was racking my brain for decoration ideas for the shower. The ribbons you enclosed saved the day. We had bought a cute paper Japanese umbrella so I tied a bunch of the ribbons on the top with streamers falling down. For the gifts we tied ribbons to it like a May-pole with a gift at the end of each. It looked very nice & everyone complimented us. Ribbon is quite scarce here anyway, so I gave lots of the pretty white ones to girls who had none for their shower gift—so we really made use of it all. A Japanese girl made nut cups & tiny parasols for table decorations. The Hotel made us a beautiful, three-tiered white cake, which we served with ice cream & coffee. We also bought flowers & cut the blossoms off & strewed them over the tables. Lois was completely surprised & never surmised a shower was in the offing. When everyone was there, Elinor casually called her up, & she soon came bouncing in, still combing her hair, skirt unfastened, & blouse unbuttoned—she thought she was going out with Bill soon. She got some lovely gifts, & everyone seemed to have a good time.

Nothing too new in Tokyo. Army Day is Tuesday, so we all have a holiday. We'll have a huge parade right across the street from the Old Kaijo.

Am going to a big formal party next Thursday so have been getting my things organized. It's a dinner-dance at the American Club for the Civil Intelligence Section.

My room girl brought me a bouquet of Camellias & Daphne this morning. The Daphne makes the whole room smell so good.

Must close & meet the girls.

> Love,
> Norma Jean

> 7 April 1948
> (A very important date, eh!)

Dear Madame President,

Congratulations, Mother darling, on your election success. I certainly do have a Mother to be proud of. I'm betting the Business & Professional Women will have an "outstandin'" year. I know you can do a good job & wish you all kinds of success. Wish I could be there to see Madame Pres. in action & help in any way I could.

Yesterday was Army Day, so American Occupation production stopped & celebration took over. They had a big parade in the morning & open house at all of the clubs in the afternoon. It was a gorgeous day & really warm. We put on our shorts & watched the parade from the roof of the Old Kaijo & got a good start on our spring tans. In the afternoon, Emilie went for a ride & shopping at a Japanese bazaar. I went to the American Club for open house. Lois & Bill wanted me to meet the Sgt. who will be best man before the wedding takes place next week, so I went with them. He was very nice. Later, we all had a turkey dinner at the Old Kaijo & went to the Ernie Pyle to see "Secret Beyond the Door"—so I had a very nice Army Day.

This evening, I'm putting the finishing touches on the things I'll wear for the party tomorrow night. The other girls were all wearing strapless formals so I made my pink one strapless too. It looks real sharp we think. Am wearing long black gloves, black earrings & necklace, & black evening bag with it. Gad, Tokyo is the most clothes conscious place I've every seen—takes all my ingenuity to keep up.

Your letters have been so good, Mom, keep re-reading them. Loved the article about kissing & pinching girls being banned.

How is Dave's Mother? Was very sorry to hear of her critical condition.

I sent a package to Larry Feb. 17th & got it back today—what a blow! I don't have his right address. Have also written him a couple letters I bet he never got. Will you let me know his right address soon? Also tell him to call for old mail at Gen'l Del., as maybe they are holding some there. His name isn't in the Bakersfield Directory, by the way, or they'd have been delivered. Don't know how I ever misplaced his address, but you know my usual confusion.

Cheers for the new B. & P. Prexy! The meeting will now be adjourned.

. Respectfully submitted,
Norma Jean Cone, Secretary

20 April 1948

Dearest Esther & Dave,

Received your wedding pictures & have practically worn them out looking at & studying them. Thanks loads; you sure had a nice selection, & I think they all came out swell. Your new home sounds good. I'm so glad you love the thrill of using all of your lovely gifts.

My mouth sure watered when you told about the dinner you gave for the folks.

Dave, I was very sorry to hear of your Mother's death. Mom told me about you all being there in her last letter.

Lois, the girl from my office was married, & I'm still recuperating. I went with them to Yokohama in the morning, where they were married at the American Consul Office. At six p.m. they were married at the 8th Cavalry Brigade Chapel. Only 5 of us were at the wedding. Then came the reception. I was hostess & in charge of all the details, so I have a vague idea of the work a wedding takes. There were 125—from Colonels to PFC's & so many Sgts. (almost out the windows). Everyone seemed to have a good time. They had a beautiful wedding cake nearly three feet high. The bride & groom just glowed with happiness all evening. Our Colonel let them use his sedan all evening, & everyone cooperated so well. They are honeymooning in Kyushu, which is lovely this time of year because of the cherry blossoms & wisteria.

If you're wondering about this stationery—it's good old rice paper. Just hope it can stand the trip.

I got the income tax form you forwarded, Esther. I was confused so went to the income tax man at the Judge Advocate's office this morning. He said our Civilian Personnel office had given us the wrong information as to forms to fill out, so he fixed it all up for me—now all I need is the $288 to pay the bill. We have until June 15th, because of being overseas.

How did Lois & Arch's vacation come out? I enjoyed Dad's letter so much telling of his being so popular at weddings—they just know a good man when they see one. You sure get a lot done Esther—wish I could loan you a couple of my maids, don't see how people live without them now. They've been bringing me the prettiest cherry blossom bouquets this week.

Am sure busy at the office keeping track of all the precious stones & metals & keeping up the old fighting spirit—didn't lose an argument all day, so at least came out with a moral victory today.

Goodnight for now, must hit the sack.

Love,
Norma Jean

30 April 1948

Dearest Mother,

Received the dress & your swell letter today. The dress is just what I had in mind. I've just finished trying it on, & it fits just right. The maid is pressing it now & am planning on wearing it tomorrow night. Thanks a million. Am enclosing a $20 money order for it.

I sent a small package for you today, Mom, cause "You've been just like a Mother To Me." The PX didn't have any cards but I do wish you a happy Mothers Day & I'll be thinking about you especially hard come May 9, mother darling.

I finally bought an Argus C-3 camera. You have to win in a lottery to buy one at the PX, & at last I had a lucky number. Now I can really take good pictures—especially color for my projector. They cost $74 in the States, but I got mine plus the flash attachment for $53. That really was a blow to my finances, as my income tax is due, but you've got to get things when you have the chance here. I'm really proud of my camera & supplies, as now I've got the slide projectors, G.E. light meter, Argus C-3 camera & two little cameras I can use for black & white when I have color in my Argus. Never thought I'd get the camera bug, but that's the chief talk in most conversations, & everyone takes pictures like mad. The PX very seldom has film that will fit my Argus; it's such a popular size that it sells out as fast as it comes in. Would you please send me some? It takes 35-mm film. I'd like some black & white & some color (Kodachrome).

Last weekend, Emilie & I went to Kyoto & Nara. We stayed at the Kyoto Hotel. It was perfectly beautiful. Most of the cherry blossoms had gone, but the wisteria, azalea & trees were gorgeous. We took sightseeing tours madly. Our entire weekend cost only $4.25 & that was for train fare (with Pullman accommodations) coming home. I went to buy our tickets going & the G.I. in Tokyo gave me our two tickets—they have no check, & he was feeling good I guess. There was no hotel bill as we were in the dormitory room, & our meals are taken from our monthly wages. With yen I bought myself a damascene bracelet like the one I sent you, some silver spoons & some ugly masks.

This noon, Emilie & I had luncheon dates. We ate at the Imperial Hotel, which is where all the wheels live—mostly Drs., Generals & Colonels. We went with some newspapermen we know. I was sure glad to go, as I've always wanted to see the place. The food was no better than any other place—just a little more class.

Never worry about my telling any man anything about my being his servant. If there's any serving to do he's going to have to hire one. I'd hate to be in Lois' position but if I were I don't think I'd stay there long. Golly, she must want to get married badly.

Those property prices seem absolutely ridiculous to me. Golly, I'm thankful we have good old "310". Sure makes me appreciate my $6 room & maid service. No wonder people are coming back after they've gone home to the States a while.

Did you read anything about the Korean-Japanese riots? The occupation forces were put on alert (also for May Day) but we didn't know anything about it until we read the *Stars & Stripes*.[27]

Must close for now. Thanks for your shopping service—I really appreciate it. All my love to my wonderful mother.

Norma Jean

---

27 Over 1,000 people were arrested.

Fourteen

Dear Mom,

The mail clerk was absent the other day when I mailed your letter so couldn't get the money order. Bet you were wondering what happened.

Had a nice May Day. All military personnel were on the alert, as they were ready for anything with the Korean riots, Russians, & labor unions all in a turmoil. It was very peaceful. We awoke to the clatter of getas & Ninjas going to the Palace Plaza. There were thousands by noontime with bands & parades all over the place. They had one big parade at about 3 o'clock then all went home.

Must close as my "crew" is here & work is waiting.

Love,
N. J. jr

13 May 1948

Dearest Esther & Dave,

Just received the delicious cookies—boy, do they ever taste good. They came through very well with not even a dent in the box. Guess it was the "Special Handling" that did it.

Have your last letter at home & think there was something I was going to answer in it but can't remember. Did you get the ashtray I sent? No, I didn't steal it. We were going through the museum in Kyoto where they had a lot of things for sale when I spotted one of the ashtrays. I sure thought of you Esther & decided I had to have one. I was strictly legal & asked the little man to sell me one. He said they were not for sale, so I gave up—but with an awfully dejected look. I was walking out in the garden a little later when he came out & asked if I was the one who wanted the ashtray. When I said yes, he pulled it out of his pocket & gave it to me. Nobody could understand why I was so tickled with it, but I knew you'd understand.

Your dinners & breakfasts sound so good. Am getting awfully anxious now to see that Bell home. Have no definite plans yet about the future, as so much depends on the world situation. Emilie & I have brainstorms all the time about what we're going to do, but they change as fast as the weather. Have been as busy as always just gadding about. Last weekend, I went to a hotel near Fuji. It rained Saturday, which made it bad for picture taking, but Sunday was nice. The eclipse was going on our way down, & it was fun to watch. Did you see it? All the Nips were out with their pieces of smoked glass.

Am getting the "Californian" regularly now & sure do like it. It makes the rounds of all the gals in the office too.

Must close for now & dash off a note to Mom telling her I got the black sandals. I sure like them & they are about the most comfortable shoes I've seen in a long time. 'Bye for now & thanks a million for the goody cookies.

All my love,
Norma Jean

13 May 1948

Dearest Mom & Dad,

I've just finished work but decided to stay & write you at least a quickie. I received the black sandals & am so happy with them. They are so comfortable I kept forgetting I had new shoes on, the first time I wore them. I think they are good looking & go so well with the clothes I have. Thanks so much. My next check will finish off my income tax & hope I have enough to send you some for the shoes.

It's been raining off & on all week. It's still chilly, & I wear skirts & sweaters all the time to work yet. We've certainly had a mild winter compared to last year. The rain will last through the middle of July, then the sweltering heat begins.

Last week, I saw the opera "Madame Butterfly". It was perfectly beautiful. The costumes & scenery were just gorgeous, & the singing was wonderful. It was at the Imperial Theatre for a week for Allied personnel only. Of course, it was an all-Japanese cast. The male lead, who was supposed to be an American Naval Officer, looked so odd at first in our Navy uniform, but after the first scene everyone got over the shock of it, as he was such a good singer.

That's a good idea not to send me any more things, Mom, unless I specially need them as I'm going to wear out the things I have this summer & next fall, so I won't have extra baggage. Egad, every time I think of packing, I shudder as I've seemed to collect so darn much junk. Have enough souvenirs for a lifetime.

Dad, you were asking about my radio. The Crosley I bought in New York has been wonderful, & I haven't had a bit of trouble with it. It's built for short wave, but so far, I haven't had the aerial fixed for short wave. I was just talking to a friend about it last week, & he's going to fix it up for me. I really enjoy the radio over here, as we have no commercials except advice to extend enlistment for service men or to save our money by buying bonds. We get all the best stateside programs & special overseas ones like Command Performance.

It's very late, as I just finished writing a note to Esther thanking her for those delicious cookies. Must close & get home before it gets dark.

All my love,
Norma Jean

16 May 1948

Dearest Folks,

It's a foggy Sunday morning & am listening to California Melodies.
Received the shoes & bag Friday. I sure like the way the bag is made. We have to carry so many cards & identification things, & the little deal in front is a perfect place to keep them. The shoes are very nice. The green ones fit swell, but the white ones are a little large. A friend, Bessie, tried them on, & they fit her perfectly so think I'll sell them to her, as they keep slipping off my heels. They're lovely shoes & so good looking—she thinks so too. She has a pair too small for her that I will buy, so we'll come out even.

I had an exciting morning yesterday. Being Saturday, I was just getting ready to go to the PX. The phone rang & a G.I. from the office asked me if I locked the door Friday when I left. I said I did & asked if something was wrong. He had a desperate tone to his voice & told me to get there as fast as I could. He sounded as though half the place had been stolen, so I practically ran all the way. When I got there M.P.'s, bank guards, & our Officer of the Day were standing around & asked me if I was sure things had been locked. I was sure & had two witnesses to prove it, so was cleared. Come to find out someone had broken in, opened our desk drawers, a supply cabinet, & turned all the lights on. They didn't take anything, & none of the safes or locked files were opened. They called the finger print man but the G.I. who discovered it had merrily touched everything already. We'll probably all be called in for a security lecture tomorrow from the Col., as he gets so excited. What a life!

Must write Larry a letter. It hardly seems possible that May 26th is almost here already.

'Bye for now. Thanks a million for the package.

Love,

Norma Jean

P.S.—I think I owe you about $35—right?

20 May 1948

Dear Esther & Dave,

Was I ever thrilled with the color slides. Could hardly wait for it to get dark that evening, so I could see them. You have such a nice selection, too. Who took them? You want them returned don't you? Our walls are painted white, so it is so handy to see them anytime with my projector.

Warm weather started all of a sudden this week. It rains off & on, but it is warm & very humid. You roast with a raincoat on & get soaked without it. Mosquitoes are starting to come, & we're all being given mosquito bars & nets for our beds this week.

We're going to have an office picnic next Wednesday afternoon. The Tokyo Military Gov't Team has $260 they don't know what to do with from their club funds, so they've invited we "Bankers" to join them. It's for all civilians, officers & EM, & they promise steak & beer. The Col. said we could close shop for the afternoon. It's going to be at Roosevelt Recreation Park—about 1/2 hour ride from Tokyo. They're planning on swimming & softball so best I start training for an athletic day.

Lois & Bill invited me to their home Tuesday. It's so cute & cozy. It's at the 7th Cav. Reg't here in Tokyo. It's a Japanese house & has lots of sliding doors & has full length sliding glass all around for windows. They have a house-boy & maid who keep the place spotless. Lois is having so much fun fixing it up & making curtains.

Now that you have your Civil Service rating, Esther, will you have to work such long hours?

Do they have seamless nylons now? Are they wearing real dark shades now? Sometimes the PX only has real dark ones & we're a little confused. If they have seamless ones let me know, because I'd like some for the summer.

Must close for now—time for Emilie to come home.

Love,
Norma Jean

24 May 1948

Dearest Mom & Dad,

Received the film in the morning's mail. Can hardly wait for a good trip, so I can take some pictures. So far am using just black & white, while I'm learning about the settings on my camera. Am just about ready to promote myself to color—am thinking of a good weekend trip & will pray for good weather. Thanks loads—will pay you next month when my income tax will have been paid.

Happy Anniversary! As usual the PX had nothing suitable for the special occasion. All they had was "Happy Mothers Day to My Wife" & somehow it just didn't seem to fit. We had a rainy weekend, but it was nice today, when everyone had to go to work. Had a quiet Sunday. Like most everyone in Tokyo I went to the PX Sunday afternoon. It's fun as people go just to meet their friends & see the newest souvenirs more than anything. I met half the office & a girl I came over on the ship with, who I hadn't seen in months.

Lois & Bill had to move Saturday. They had just been in their house 11 days. A Capt. decided he'd like it, so there was nothing they could do but go. Lois called Saturday morning & asked if I'd help. I helped all afternoon & evening. We had loads of fun. Another Sgt. & I polished furniture until we practically had calluses. We ended up by even giving my shoes a furniture polish job as the directions said something about it not harming leather. Don't think my old moccasins will ever be anything but a dull & drab brown, which refuses any polish or shine. Their new house isn't as nice as their old one, & Bill was so disgusted. Lois didn't mind but dreaded the ordeal of moving again.

Mom, am sending a present for your birthday tomorrow. Please let me know if anything is broken. It's kind of an experiment, too, to see if it can be mailed successfully. If it breaks I can get more, so let me know. Don't think it will be there on time, but you'll know it's on the way.

Am feeling so good lately. Have lost a little weight I guess, because my clothes all seem big for me. Must have been what I needed as I've honestly never felt better.

All my love to you,
Norma Jean

Fifteen

5 June 1948

Dearest Mamasan,

Happy Birthday, Mother darling. I sure got fouled up with your package this year, & I feel badly that it won't get there in time. The P.O. said it rattled, so I had to wait until I could get back to the main PX to have it re-packed. My thoughts have been with you all day & hope you had a good day.

Will send the color slides back with this letter, so you'll have them for your vacation. Also, I want to give Lois & Archie something. I will send it home if you don't mind, because I don't know about customs, & I would rather leave the price tags on to be sure. It's just a little luncheon set.

We had quite an earthquake night before last. It happened in the wee hours of the morning & woke everyone up. It didn't scare me a bit because it wasn't the jerky kind—just a gentle swaying which lasted quite a while.

Have been hearing so much about the floods in the Pacific Northwest. It must be pretty terrific.

I was glad to see that ad about opera glasses. I didn't know if I was getting a bargain or not when I bought them. Think I'll get more for "presents" when I go home.

The PX had some silk like Mrs. Fanshiers sample several months ago, but I haven't seen any since. They might have some on the Ginza though. How much does she want? If I get it in the PX you have to buy about six yards, but in Jap stores you can buy just what you want.

Your vacation plans sound so exciting. What are the dates you'll be there—think you already told me once.

My writing is worse than usual. Am writing in bed. Am trying to beat a cold this week & so am staying right in bed. Am kind of weak & tired but otherwise okay. The little room girls love to take care of us. Yesterday, they gave me a massage. They flutter around & keep straightening the blankets & want me to take "aspiling" (aspirin). Had breakfast in bed this morning. It's a gorgeous day so think I'll go on the roof in the sun in a little while.

Esther has been writing the nicest letters & sending the cutest packages. She's such a wonderful sister. She really sounds happy, & I'm so glad.

Has Erwin Ross come home yet? Some friends of Bessie's came up from the Philippines this week, & we've been showing them the sights of Tokyo. According to them, conditions there aren't too good.

My work is rather quiet now. We have a new Col. again, & we're just waiting for his brainstorms.

Emilie just got over a cold & went away for the weekend. We sure get along well. This is her third summer in Tokyo. She's studying Mandarin Chinese madly. She wants to go to school in China now. She wanted me to, too, but more education I can't see—especially in a place where fighting is going on. An awful lot of people are going home by way of Europe, & that's still what I'd give anything to do.

I don't think I ever told you about the outcome of our office picnic. It was a gorgeous afternoon, & the park was beautiful. The enlisted men played the officers in baseball & lost nine to five. We had charcoal broiled steaks a la Col. Sterling. The old boy worked like a dog all afternoon on them, & they were scrumptious. I get so disgusted with these wives. Rank doesn't mean much to the men, but you should be with the wives—ugh! The Colonel's wife is nice, & the Sergeant's wife is nice, so I just ignore the rest at this point—can't be bothered with their silly ideas. When they saw the Colonel's wife & me having such a good time, they suddenly warmed up—but I didn't to them.

Must close before you have eyestrain.

Love,
Norma Jean

June 8, 1948

Dearest Esther & Dave,

Jeepers, feel like a heel! Have gotten those delicious goodies & haven't even acknowledged them. Those banana flakes have really been a blessing from heaven. Have had quite a bout with a cold, & all the food tastes awful. My throat was so sore, & their usually awful tasting ice cream really is good with banana flakes added. Have all the food you sent lined up beside my bed on the table. Dates are wonderful—never get them here. We do get cheese but just the kind in bottles, & this tasted awfully good. Don't think I ever thanked you for those cheese French fries—ate 'em the day they came! Thanks loads for everything, kiddo!

You asked about magazines. It's very hard to get any—the PX sells out as fast as they come, but Emilie gets an awful lot from home & says I'm to use them as much as I want, so I do okay. She seldom gets "Life" tho, & I would like any copies of that—dates matter not.

You know Irene of Silverado Canyon—have been racking my brain to think of her last name but can't. Anyhoo—met a Major Holdsworth who knows her too—he couldn't think of her last name either. He thinks he was there the same weekend we all were, as he lived there awhile. If you see her, give her my regards, & ask about Major Holdsworth. Oh, yes, please tell me her last name—this is maddening. The Major is on Okinawa & in Tokyo just for business a few days.

Heard about the Compton Invitational Track meet. It was the big subject of the daily "sportscope" over the radio.

You sound like the Bell household is really under control. Oops—here's Fibber McGee on the radio so must listen in.

Love, Norma Jean

After reading this over, you'll probably need a translation—such writing. P.S. a la Aunt Lou—have nearly worn the buttons off that pink dress—it's just right for the season now—can wear black or white with it.

15 June 1948

Dearest Folks,

Feel like a new person this week—& that's good! In my last letter I was "feeling mighty low". After three days, I called the visiting nurse. I thought it was a cold but felt so weak & tired & couldn't get over it like I should, if it were a cold. The nurse said I had a fever & called the Dr. He said I had a throat infection. He gave me penicillin for two days, & my appetite & pep came back like a flash. Saturday, I got a new permanent, & Sunday, I got a tan on the roof, so when I went to work Monday I looked so darn healthy everyone thought I had been on a vacation instead of sick leave—no sympathy at all!

Mom, I got your nice Boulder Dam letter & the nylons! Sure was glad to hear of your trip.[28] I think it's wonderful how "youse" is getting around. Just love those nylons! Emilie said her mom just sent her some, but Lois said she'd love to have some. She & Bill have been so nice to me that I'd appreciate it if you'd get some for her. She wears size 9 & would like about 4 pairs—let me know how much they are.

It's so sticky hot now. It rained this morning which helped for a while, but it's awfully sticky this evening again.

Have led such a quiet life all week that there's not even much news. Emilie & I are planning a vacation next month—we hope to go to Korea for about 10 days. Lots of red tape to go through first, though.

Good night. Must close for now & take gooood care of yourselves.

All my love,
Norma Jean

---

28 The original name for the Hoover Dam near Las Vegas, Nevada.

21 June 1948

Dearest Folks,

It's Monday evening & another week is beginning. Got paid today so will enclose a forty-dollar money order. I got a swell package of magazines from Esther Bell, which I'm eager to read tonight, too. The summer monsoon season is here now. It rains every day & will until about the middle of July. I rather like it, as it's not too hot this way— also keeps "that smell" of hot Tokyo away.

Had a very nice weekend. Saturday, 25 of us had a sukiyaki party at an On-Limits Geisha house. The food was luscious, & it was all very nice. It was John's birthday, & I got the birthday cake & food at the commissary. We had sukiyaki served with raw eggs, rice, tea, Coca-Cola, cake & peanuts. I'll cook some sukiyaki when I get home—don't know whether I've been here too long or not, but I sure like it. Of course, you have to sit on the floor & eat with chopsticks to make it real good.

Yesterday, we went shopping for Japanese phonograph records. I'm going to send some home soon—sure hope they make the trip okay.

Life at the bank goes on as usual—nothing new. You remember Col. Murray who was found guilty of stealing diamonds from the bank? He was in the other day. He's at Sugamo Prison in Japan yet. The board of officers working on our records found another discrepancy so called him in from prison for a statement. The old boy looks much older & thinner than when I last saw him.

Darn, ran out of ink again. The big Fourth of July weekend is coming up. We haven't planned anything special. Will probably watch MacArthur review the troops.

Must close for now,
Love, Norma Jean

28 June 1948

Dearest Folks,

Seems like I'm always writing you on Monday evenings. I went right to the beauty shop here at the hotel after work tonight & had a shampoo & set for my new permanent. Met Emilie at dinner, so it was rather late when I finally got to room 424.

I really did enjoy the letter I got from you today, Mom. Your vacation plans are really something this year. Where is everyone going to stay in Spokane? Was so glad you straightened me out on Archie's relatives. I never had it straight when I was in California. Bet you'll have lots of fun traveling together.

Emilie & I want to start for Korea on July 10th. Wow, the red tape we have to cut yet makes us wonder if we'll make it. We were not allowed to go there on leave because of the tense political situation, but it was re-opened again about two weeks ago. You have to have people already there make your billeting arrangements, then possibly a character check to be sure of your reason for going. We have our boat reservations already, thank goodness.

Golly, imagine 3000 UCLAns graduating. Am glad I was in no such mass movement.

Oh, yes, I have a minor problem, Mr. Anthony. Am enclosing a card from Albert Ross I got a few days ago.[29] He didn't use my right address, so it had to come thru the Japanese postal system, as you can see. Should I answer it? Frankly I don't know what I'd have to say in a "long letter" to him. Also, I'd like to know more about his "condition" before I started anything. What do you think? Have been wondering about Erwin & was glad you cleared it up in the letter. Too bad I missed him, but he probably shares my dislike for looking people up. No, I don't know the Kidder's in Yokohama. The only ones I've met in the State Department are in Tokyo & that was at that party I told you about. The State Dept Officials are quite the elite here, they think. What a vicious sounding mood I'm in. Anyhoo—is Erwin coming back or does he intend to stay in America?

---

29 Albert Ross probably was a relative of the cousin Erwin Ross with whom Jean had quite a bit to do in a later overseas assignment. Erwin Ross had been a Japanese prisoner in Manila during WWII.

I don't think I could ever keep up with you. You all sound so busy & have so much company. I'd certainly be a stranger to Dave's family. That was sure cute of Esther & Dave giving a Father's Day breakfast.

Last weekend, I saw "Les Miserables" at the British Theatre & "I Remember Mama" at the Tokyo outdoor theatre. They were both very good I thought. Emilie & I are trying to make reservations for the 3 day 4th of July weekend but without much luck so far. In Tokyo, they'll have another parade with MacArthur there.

What should I do about voting? How does one get an absentee ballot?

Golly, it gets so late so early. Now I'm sleepy. Sure hope this gets home before your vacation. Hope you both are feeling good. Have a wonderful time. Say hello to everyone for me. I think I must owe them all letters. Would love to be at the wedding. With Dad in there pitching, it should be a good omen for any marriage.

'Bye now & have fun!

All my love, Norma
Jean

Tues morning at the bank—

Did you read about the earthquake we had yesterday.[30] Kanazawa, the worst hit, is about 12 hours by train from here. I was having a shampoo at the time & didn't feel a thing.

---

30 The death toll for the earthquake was 3,700.

Sixteen

Dear Esther & Dave,

It seems like a long time since I've written you—I guess it has been. Esther, I meant to write you a "Happy Birthday" letter, but jeepers the time suddenly flew by. Was glad you liked the blouse. It sure did get there fast—ah, this efficient postal service. "Happy Birthday" to you too Dave. Why doesn't somebody tell me these things? Next year I'll send two birthday blouses.

Your entertaining really sounds nice. You always sound so busy & Happy.

Emilie & I were going to Korea July 10th, but due to the red tape of getting into that country, we'll have to wait about a month for approvals from Korea & our personnel sections. This 4th of July weekend, we finally got reservations at a Japanese hotel south of Tokyo on the Inland Sea. We're planning on leaving Sat. morning & coming back Monday.

Went swimming for the first time this season yesterday at Meiji pool after work. It had been hot & sticky all day, so the water really felt good. In the evening, we went to the American Club. Just as we were leaving, about 10:30, we heard fire engines & saw a red glow in the sky. We jumped into the car & went. A building on the main street leading out of Tokyo was burning like a box. Their fire equipment is really in sad shape & their policemen don't know how to handle crowds. They saved the two Allied buildings on each side of it, however, so guess they were a success.

The night before we (Emile & I & some newspaper friends) stayed in Radio Tokyo until 2 a.m. watching figures come in from the earthquake. It was really interesting. We met all the big name correspondents. You remember Ernest Hobrecht? He wrote "Tokyo Romance", & they had an article about it in Life. He was there—nothing like I expected, just a quiet, rather serious person. More fun—we all had delicious steak sandwiches about 1 a.m.

Am rather worn out tonight & have a big weekend coming, so must close for now.

Love,

N.J.

6 July 1948

Dearest Mom, Dad, & all,

I do hope you've had a nice trip north, folks. Bet it was fun. Am anxious to hear about your trip & everyone but realize how busy you'll be so won't expect any long letters—just have a good time.

Emilie & I had the most glorious 4th of July weekend. We left Tokyo at 9 o'clock Saturday morning. We arrived in Nagoya at 4 that afternoon. At 5:10 we got a Japanese train & after three changes & some walking, arrived at our hotel in Futami at 9:30 p.m. Boy, were we a sight when we got there. It was terribly hot & sticky all day. We rode in windowless coal trains, & we practically had Nips sitting on our laps on their crowded trains. Oh, yes, it was raining on our final hike to the hotel. We didn't think anything could be worth this effort, but one look at our hotel, & we changed our minds. It was honestly the most gorgeous spot in Japan I think. We were the only Americans in the hotel & really had super service. We had two large Japanese style rooms & a small veranda with wicker chairs & table. The hotel was beautiful—just spotless. It is located on a peninsula right on the bay. Hills covered with evergreen trees go right down to the blue, blue water. We brought our own food & had them cook it. Sunday, we saw the local sights—famous rocks & shrines, & the little village. In the afternoon we went out in the bay in a boat. It was so good, we came back & took another ride later. We watched the sun set from our veranda & just hated to think of leaving the next day. We had eaten everything we brought at this point, except our rice, so finished off in real Japanese fashion for breakfast—rice & tea.

We got the 7:18 train & arrived back in Tokyo at about 7 last night. We were so proud of ourselves as it was the first time we'd gone to a Japanese hotel far away without someone along who could speak Japanese. The manager knew about as much English as we did Japanese, but we all boned up madly, & it was surprising how much we could say to each other. We're planning on taking a few days off & going there again.

They changed the yen exchange rate. When I first got here it was fifteen yen for one dollar, then changed to fifty yen for one dollar. This weekend, it was changed to 270 yen for one dollar—which gives you an idea of their inflation. Before the war, they said it was 3 or 4 for one dollar.

Golly, is it ever hot & sticky now. We practically melted at the Bank today. I went down to the vaults awhile where it's like an icebox & got cooled off but was just that much hotter when I came up again.

Oh, forgot to tell you about the hotel's prices. It only cost ¥400 for both of us which included service & room rent for the whole time.

We had to postpone our trip to Korea. Now we think maybe we'll go in August. I found out we had to wait for 3 weeks for approval after all other arrangements had been made so couldn't make it in July.

Am sending a wooden box with phonograph records home tomorrow. Sure hope they make it. It's going regular mail so will probably be a long time.

In Futami, for a souvenir, we bought the cutest masks. They're red, black & gold with white feathers. The mouth opens & you can make the ears wiggle.

Must close for tonight. Give my best wishes to everyone. Put some extra lipstick on & give the groom a kiss for me. Hoping this finds everyone well.

All my love,
Norma Jean

12 July 1948

Dear Esther & Dave,

Just a note this evening while I sit here trying to keep cool. Received the nicest letter from Mom this morning. She sounded so excited about their trip, & I don't blame her.

Everyone seems to be competing for the best tans in our office—most came in with terrific burns today. I spent the weekend with Lois & Bill. Saturday, we went horseback riding & for a long ride. Sunday, Lois fixed waffles for breakfast, which really tasted good. In the afternoon, we went with some other people out to Chiba peninsula along the ocean & had a picnic. Emilie went to Zushi with some of her friends & came home with a good sunburn.

I sent some phonograph records home a few days ago. They went regular mail, registered. I sent it to myself & marked it as personal property so there shouldn't be any customs—let me know if there is. Do you have a record player? If you do, go ahead & play the records. Most are weird sounding but I like some—especially "Shina No Yoru." Sure hope they don't break.

We were supposed to have a picnic Wednesday afternoon, but the General decided he'd come for an inspection that day, soooo we're cleaning the place up like mad. Tomorrow, we have the floors waxed.

Your new car sounds like a wonderful idea, Esther. The Bell's seem to be really branching out.

Must close & starch clothes—the little girls just can't understand why we want them starched so never do it when they wash.

> All my love,
> Norma Jean

20 July 1948

Dear Folks,

Hope this will be waiting for you when you get back home. Will be anxious to hear about your vacation.

We had another office picnic last week. It was very hot, so we went in the swimming pool. After about an hour, it started to thunder &

lightning. We had to quit swimming, & it really poured. We were all soaked when we roasted hot dogs over the fire—but it was lots of fun.

The day before the picnic, the General came to inspect the bank. We "shaped up" all week, & the place really looked nice. The funniest thing happened. We were told he was on his way & so we're expecting him. All of a sudden we heard a yell in the next room. It sounded exactly like someone had slipped on our new-waxed floors. A couple of the men started in to pick up the pieces when we found out the General had come, & our Lieutenant Colonel had just called attention. Guess he was a little excited—sure sounded like "oops" to us.

Sunday, the American Club had a party at Nagai Beach. It was real fun. Got a swell tan; boy, did some come back with bad burns. For lunch, they served sandwiches, salad, cokes & cookies. For supper we had chicken, ham, salad, corn, beans, rolls & chocolate jelly rolls. They brought chefs & waiters, & it was really swell to be served right on the beach.

Now, our plans for Korea are set for August 14—red tape has been cut, & we should make it.

Gee, the news from Europe sounds critical.[31] Every time I see some of our Russian "allies" here, I wonder what's going on in their little brains.

Got the cutest letter from Yvonne while she was at our house drinking lemonade & watching the people sewing. I could just picture it & would have loved to kibitz & drink some of that lush stuff.

Have been listening to Fibber McGee & Bob Hope while writing this, so you may not understand any goofy sentences.

'Bye for now—
Love, Norma Jean

P.S.—Lois & Bill have been wanting one of those little washing machines—the kind that sits on the sink & holds about two sheets. They don't know where they could send for one. Could you find out & tell me? She thinks they're around $35.

Love,
Norma Jean

---

31 The Soviets blockaded West Berlin and on June 26th, 1948, the United States and Britain started an airlift to provide food, fuel, medicine, and water. The airlift lasted 11 months.

Seventeen

6 August 1948

Dearest Folks,

Was I ever glad to get your nice vacation letter. Seemed so long between letters, but I know how busy you were. Was so glad to hear news of everyone in Oregon & Wash.

Have I ever been busy lately. Meant to write last week, but all I can remember of last week is dashing madly to the beach, Yokohama, shows, dinners, etc. Everyone I know seemed to have a brainstorm about going places. Friends from Okinawa came this week, which fixed things up but good. Tomorrow, I'm going to Lake Yamanaka, Sunday to Nagai Beach, Monday to school & pack for Korea, Tuesday a farewell party for John, Wednesday we board the ship for Korea. Am looking forward to a restful three-day voyage before our sightseeing begins.

Have been having quite a time at the office lately & will be so glad to get away from that madhouse awhile. A new Major came & started a "revolution". Nothing suited him, & he got so excited. He's calmed down now, & we're getting along—only had a minor argument with him today. He's a funny fellow—to hear him, you'd think he would love nothing better than to send you home on the next ship, but he just likes to argue. After one of our better arguing days, he introduced me to his wife & daughter as one of his ablest assistants—what a life! Since then he's given everyone lots more to do & me less, so I feel I won.

It's awfully hot & sticky, but we've had thunder showers often. There's been heat lightning every night.

Got a nice thank you note from Gordon Solie for sending him the stamps. He wants to know about the price so will write him.

Lois got her stockings you sent me & likes them—thanks. Think we broke about even on that Mom, eh? Thanks for enclosing the UCLA magazines, etc. Tell Esther I received the "Life" magazines & really enjoyed them. Was sorry to hear of Dave's skin troubles. Hope the treatment & diet help.

How is Larry? It's been so long since I've heard anything from him & I've been wondering so much what he's doing & how he is lately.

Have been thinking about going to Okinawa for the rest of my contract. Have been offered a job there. Would be able to save more money & be closer to China, which would help in that expense. Am trying to decide before I start the red tape involved in transferring. Emilie is thinking of going to Hong Kong in October. She may take a job of writing for a paper there. We're both in a quandary. Hate to think of breaking up our Cone-Graf organization.

Oh, yes, we all got a raise. The same one Esther got plus 25% for overseas duty. They're going to start charging us 7¢ a meal more for food & $2.57 a month for maid service which will take part of it away again. I don't see how working girls living away from home in the States could manage—gad, I can't even get ahead over here.

Have been wanting to talk to you lately on the phone so think I may call home after I come back from Korea. Tell me if there's any particular time that would be best. It's always so good to hear your voices again.

Must close for now. There will be 15 of us going to the lake tomorrow, & I'm supposed to get some snacks lined up tonight. Will try to write more soon—maybe on that 3 day boat trip.

All my love,
Norma Jean

P.S. Tuesday, Okinawa deal is all off. Decided it wouldn't be worth the red tape & effort. Are all ready to board the Army Transport "Brewster" for Korea tomorrow at 9 a.m.

12 August 1948

Aboard the U.S.A.T. General Brewster

Dearest Mom, Dad, Esther, Dave & Larry,

We boarded the ship yesterday at 9 a.m. & sailed right on schedule at 11 a.m. It's a beautiful ship, very large & not many people. We have the choice room as it's the only one with three port holes. There are four bunks, closets & a bath & shower we share with a girl next door. We have one other girl in with us. She's very nice & is from the States on her way to Korea, too.

The weather is hot, but there is always a nice breeze. The sea is calm but quite a roll this morning. Are we ever enjoying the meals—delicious. Had forgotten how good ice cream could be, as Japanese ice cream is lousy. Last night after dinner, we saw "My Wild Irish Rose" on the top deck. It was gorgeous there—lots of stars out, a mild warm breeze & comfortable lounge chairs. After that, we played Bingo in the main deck lounge—didn't win a thing.

There are quite a few dependents with children going home to the States. The little darlings are driving the mess help mad. There are one hundred officers going to Korea too. Most are young 2nd Lts. straight from the Academy. They're all quite excited. Emilie & I are the only Civilian women that got on at Yokohama. They can't understand why we want to go to Korea for a vacation—must have heard the rumors of conditions there.

Saturday morning
We're scheduled to dock at Jinsen this noon.[32]

We've been passing hundreds of little islands all morning. One was especially picturesque, as it has a large building that looks like a monastery built on top of it. Yesterday evening, it was quite foggy but it's bright & hot this morning. The sea has been just like glass the last two days. We were told yesterday that our meals will cost 57¢ each. So at the most all we will have to pay for the trip will be $5.70.

Jinsen is about an hour's drive from Seoul they say so will be there this afternoon. Am taking lots of pictures. More later.

---

32 Jinsen was the name used by the Japanese who ruled Korea from 1905 to 1945--now referred to as Incheon or Inchon.

Monday morning

The weekend is over, so while our friends are slaving away, Emile &
I are doing our cleaning & are all set for some sight seeing.

We went ashore at 2 o'clock Saturday afternoon. A Col. & his girl
friend were waiting to meet us. They drove us to Seoul, which took
about an hour. The Col. is a friend of Emilie's, as he works in her
section & comes to Tokyo once in a while.

Wednesday afternoon

This is about the tenth time I've sat down to write, but something
always stopped me.

To get back where I left off, Sunday was a big day for Korea, as you
probably have heard. South Korea celebrated their independence all
day. In the morning, we went to see Rhee inaugurated. It was held on
the Capital grounds. To get in, Koreans had to have invitations. They
let all Americans in. MacArthur & his wife arrived about 11:20 amid
screaming M.P. Jeeps & mounted tanks.

Friday afternoon

What a life—can't even finish what I started to say. Anyhoo—MacArthur arrived at the inauguration. Rhee made a long speech, which we, of course, couldn't understand, & it seemed Koreans had trouble, too. It was terribly hot & little shade. MacArthur also talked, but the P. A. system was weak, & we couldn't hear what he was saying. The Koreans celebrated the rest of the day & night. They had parades & more parades, & in the evening they decorated the streetcars like floats & paraded them. Everyone was ready for riots, which was probably why there were none.

All the service men carry pistols with them all the time. The Korean police all carry big guns & have gun emplacements in front of the police stations.

We're living at North Mountain Apartments. We have two bedrooms, a living room, dinette, kitchen (no stove or refrigerator), & both the girls who live here permanently have theirs fixed up very nicely.

Monday & Tuesday, Emilie & I saw Seoul via foot & bus routes. We went shopping, but the PX had nothing, & the prices in the little shops were terrific. We bought some Yuan at 50 to one dollar, but since the black market rate is from 400 Yuan to 1000 Yuan to $1 we didn't get far.

We can't get over the attitude of the natives. It's so different from the Japanese. They tell you frankly & really have tempers. If they don't want their picture taken they may throw a rock at you, but at least you know where you stand. They're about 200 years behind civilization.

Women work on road gangs with the men. The small children don't wear any clothes & are filthy. The native costume is pretty on the women—full skirts & little jackets. The women carry bundles on their heads & have beautiful posture & carriage. Their clothes look so clean, & you can't see how they do it. They live in shacks. They wash & iron by beating the clothes.

Last night, some friends of mine took us to some wealthy Koreans' for dinner. It was delicious—American style food. We had hors d'oeurvres, wine, fried shrimp with mashed potatoes, chicken, carrots, beans, peas, boiled potatoes, rolls, butter, apple pie, ice cream & coffee. They live in a western-style house & had the most gorgeous silverware I've ever seen.

This morning, we drove out to the King's tomb. It's north of Seoul & they say only about 10 miles from the 38th parallel. On our way out I saw a gruesome sight. They were hanging a dog. Children were standing around watching. They were also carrying one away which had already been broiled & was ready for dinner. The King's tomb was a pretty place & well kept.

The roads are horrible as soon as you get off main streets, & in a Jeep they're murder.

In the city, the main streets are nice & wide, & they have some nice buildings. The people live along narrow alleys with houses stacked on each other. They eat a lot of garlic & pepper, so you can imagine the smells.

Oh, yes, we have water part of the time & hot water about twice a day. You never know when the electricity is on or off. The Russians cut it off about 9 o'clock every night then our generators take over. All lights have to be out at 11 o'clock.

They have evacuated dependents from here already, & civilians are next. Most of the girls will be coming to Tokyo to work.

We have one maid. She's an older woman who says nothing but okay, washee, & goodnight. If she wants to tell you something she goes thru all sorts of pantomime. She was all excited yesterday & kept bouncing around & pointing. There was a fire a couple of blocks away. We went to it, which seemed to please her. When she irons, she spreads a blanket on the floor & squats over to iron. The ironing board still hasn't been used. She seems to have a fascination with the bathroom. She's there all the time unless we tell her something to do. She cleans the plumbing every time we use it & runs water to fill buckets & the bathtub in case the water is turned off. We've decided she just isn't used to the modern fixtures.

Monday morning

This is our last day in Seoul. We'll get the train for Pusan tomorrow morning.

We really hate to leave yet, as it's been so interesting, & everyone has been so nice to us.

Saturday we went to a wedding. The bride & groom are from Hawaii, but of Korean origin. The groom's father flew from Hawaii for the occasion. They were married in the Chong Dong Methodist Church. The bride looked lovely; I took lots of pictures. The reception was held in Seoul's best Chinese restaurant. We had toasts to the couple then all sorts of Chinese food—delicious. Practically everyone there was from Hawaii except us & the Koreans. They had an Hawaiian orchestra & hula dances. Had a wonderful time.

Have been packing this morning & now it's time for lunch, so must close, as I do want to get this mailed today. Pardon the stationery, but it was the handiest thing when I started out.

Hope this finds you all well. More later.

All my love,
Norma Jean

August 28, 1948

Dearest Folks,

We arrived back in Tokyo last night at 7 p.m. We would have liked to stay in Korea a little longer, but now that we're back it seems awfully nice.

We left Seoul Tuesday morning & arrived at Pusan (also called Fusan) that evening. It was a hot, dusty trip. We went through lots of tunnels, & with the train's coal smoke we looked about three shades darker after each one. The scenery was pretty though. Korea is a mountainous country & we followed the valley, which looked so picturesque with the farm villages & streams. Pusan is pretty but oh, so dirty. We stayed at the railway hotel. At night we looked out over the grounds in front & saw thousands of people sleeping. Many are refugees just returned from Japan, Manchuria, or China & who have no homes. Wednesday, we took in the sights around the city via foot & Jeep. The coastline is beautiful there, & I took several color pictures—sure hope they come out.

We got up at 5:30 Thursday to catch the 6 a.m. ship for Japan. It was a rainy, stormy morning. The ship was even rolling tied up at the dock. All I've got to say is just never worry about my getting seasick. If that ride didn't do it, nothing ever will. Emilie & I were the only ones not sick. We slept part of the way although it was hard to keep in the bunk. There were only nine passengers. A nurse was in the cabin with us. She's been all over & never sick before, but she just lay there & kept moaning & groaning, wishing she'd die & then make another quick dash for the bucket outside. Emilie & I were famished at lunch & dinner. The others who were able to be up & see us all turned about 3 shades greener when we asked for another order of sandwiches. We were four hours late because of the storm, so missed our train. We were glad, because we had a wonderful time looking around Hakata the next morning. We got the train at 4 o'clock Friday afternoon & arrived in Tokyo at 7 Saturday night. We both agreed it was the best vacation we've taken.

Am anxious to go to the office tomorrow for mail. Also, they say there have been lots of changes in personnel since I left. It's a beautiful morning & we're going to the beach so must close. More later.

Love,
Norma Jean

31 August 1948

Dearest Mom & Dad,

Received the most wonderful letters from "310". I was so happy to have a letter waiting for me when I got home from Korea. Esther wrote a nice one too & sent a package of scrumptious looking cheese.

Ah, life's little problems. Yesterday afternoon at work my right ear started to ache. By evening, it was swollen & hurting more. I went to the Dr., & he packed it with medicated cotton & told me to apply heat to it. I kept the hot water bottle on it all night, but this morning it felt much worse. I went back to the Dr. this morning, & he said I had an infection. He gave me a shot of penicillin & some pills for pain & said to come back tomorrow. The medicine took effect in about an hour, & I went to work. My ear & jaw feel numb but don't hurt any more. He said to apply more heat, so am planning a quiet evening tonight. Sure am glad I went to him right away, as he said it's mostly in the outer ear, so I don't think it will be hard to clear up. We have good medical service & the Drs. all seem to be good.

Was glad to hear Dave's skin irritation is improving. Have they decided what caused it? They sure have had skin diseases here—much is caused from malnutrition they say.

Emilie & I are still enthused about our Korea vacation. Can hardly wait for the pictures to be developed. We agree perfectly on traveling, & she's so nice to be with. We always agree on things we want to do & see. We've decided we can't break up the Graf-Cone organization yet. I've decided against leaving Tokyo, & she's going to stay until Jan. or Feb. too. We have a wonderful idea for another vacation now. We want to go to the Philippines in December. Think we can make it, as we learned the channels last time. I have a friend who makes reservations on ships, so that will solve transportation. Will probably stop at several islands & probably Shanghai. We want to take about a month off. I have the leave coming, & so does she. She's already asked her office &, since she's staying longer, she can go. I may stay a month longer too, so I can go. Doesn't that sound good? If Irwin Ross is there, give me his address, & I'll look him up. Esther was also asking about my future plans. They change constantly, but we'd like to go to China next spring, but our plans are still in the unorganized stage.

Lois quit work last week. She's rather fragile & it was quite a strain to work & be a homemaker at the same time. She also just found out that she will be a mamasan next spring. I'm the only one she's told at the office, & we've had lots of fun with "our" secret. She & Bill are so nice to me & are always wanting me to stay with them over weekends, etc. Bill is regular army, & Lois likes the army life, so they're both so happy. He's a Mess Sergeant, & we always have luscious food at their house.

We're supposed to get paid tomorrow so will send some money for the insurance. Also, will send some extra. Would you please buy me a pair of shoes, purse & gloves? I want to wear them with navy blue as I've had a two-piece suit & a navy dress made. Any color you think would look nice with navy will be fine. I'd like heels, not flats, for shoes.

I've never heard of that customs deal on records before. People said they thought it would go smoother if I addressed them to myself. I'm sorry it was such a nuisance. Thanks loads for taking care of it so well. I was sure wondering if they'd get there in one piece. Have you heard them yet?

Was glad to hear of news of Jill. Gee, she's really having a time. How I'd like to loan her a couple of maids—she's the one who should be having the service.

Must close as it's time for a pill & the heat treatment.

Love,
Norma Jean

Eighteen

5 Sept. 1948

Dearest Esther,

Did I ever appreciate your letter that was waiting when I returned from Korea. It seemed ages since I had news from the States during the holiday. Also got the delicious cheese & magazines last week—thanks a million, kiddo. You're always so good to me.

Emilie & I just got home from church. We hadn't gone for such a long time & really enjoyed it. Helen Keller is here now & will speak at the Chapel tomorrow night--think I'll go. This is the long Labor-Day weekend, & we slipped by not taking a trip. We were gone when reservations were being made, however, so decided to stay in town. We both had dates last night. I'm going to visit Lois & Bill, & tomorrow take in Tokyo's celebration. Also, because of my aching ear I decided best I don't plan too much. It is almost well now, have only had one minor relapse today, so feel confident I'll recover. I had penicillin shots, took pills, & Friday, he gave me an ear wash & drugs, & said no more penicillin was necessary. One of our maids was a nurse during the war & she's taken a delight in treating my case. Every evening, when I come home she washes my ear out, puts the drops in & gives me a super massage. I also have a fungus infection on my feet, which I'm treating, & it's improving lots. The Dr. thinks I probably got it in my ear from the foot infection. He said it's a rather mild form & they have lots of it here & know just

192

what to do for it now. Have been wondering about Dave's dermatitis. Hope he's feeling all right. Sure am glad the Dr. found a treatment that helped him.

It's been rather cool last week, but yesterday & today it's been so sultry & hot that you're wet from perspiration all the time. The rains should start before too long, & I'll be glad the heat's over.

You made me drool talking about grapes. We don't have any. The Japanese have them & they look luscious but we're not supposed to eat them. I did buy some of their peaches & plums, & they were luscious. I don't buy anything that you can't peel or that grows near the ground—too many weird diseases, & once you've seen their irrigation & fertilization system you're not even tempted.

You asked about Japanese Tea sets for the lady at the P.O. They're just beginning to get some in the PX but never have much of a selection. They cost from $12 to $25 usually. The beautiful ones are sold in Jap. stores or factories. I haven't priced them lately, but they usually run from ¥4000-¥7000, which would be at least $20 (¥5400 for $20 exchange) plus customs. I'll be glad to get her one if she wants. Also, tell me about any color she'd like. You mentioned chartreuse, red & black. The Nips don't use those colors too much. They use an orange color a lot, lots of browns & beiges, bright blues & pastels. I'm still planning on seeing China before I come home, & I was wondering if she'd rather have a Chinese set—I don't know much about the prices in China, but I could find out--which reminds me, I'm going to buy mostly linens when I get there, because they're gorgeous & lots less expensive than here. Would you & Mom be thinking what kinds you'd like & let me know before I go—months off--I know but a nice thing to think about. If I bring it home with me, I probably won't have to pay customs as we're allowed $400 duty free.

You were right about the clothes situation, Esther. Am wearing out the things I have. Lots of the gals have the "new look", but I was in the old school this summer. Have found a good dressmaker & she's made me a few "new looks" for date dresses, etc. Must close for now.

All my love,
Norma Jean

P.S. Will try to get Faye's package sent next week. Will send it to you, as I don't want her to have to pay the customs. Oh, yes, I got a letter from Sarah Kilgore. She's in Arabia as a bacteriologist for the American Arabian Oil Co. Will send you her letter when I answer it. Forgot something else. They've closed approvals for trips to Korea, so we just made it.

18 September 1948

Dearest folks,

Got the "bestest" letter from 310 today. I re-read it tonight & enjoyed it all over again. You sure are busy people, but it all sounds like so much fun. I really drooled when you talked about the food you've been having.

We've just gotten over a typhoon. It was a wonderful one. However, it did quite a bit of damage, I hear. It was more violent than last year's. It rained & rained & blew & blew. The air was so warm that it really felt good. We let our Japanese help go at 2 o'clock yesterday afternoon, as many of the train lines & electricity were going off. Today was about the most beautiful I've ever seen in Tokyo. Everything just glistened from the washing & blowing it had. The sun was bright as could be; there was the nicest gentle warm breeze & the sky was so clear you could see Mt. Fuji.

Emilie & I are going to Ikaho, a mountain resort, for the weekend, & I've just finished packing. Bet it will be beautiful again tomorrow.

Have been so busy lately. A friend from Korea was here last week & Emile & I knocked ourselves out to entertain him, as he was so nice to us there. "Madame Butterfly" was on at the Imperial Theatre, & I saw it again—really good. Also saw "Life With Father", which I liked too.

Work goes on as usual. The Major & I have our daily arguments—he's decided the Sgt & I are his advisory board. About all I do is pass the work out to the others & "discuss" the situation. Fun but gets boring. A typist brought me flowers all last week. They were zinnias, & she said from her sister's garden. Next month, says she, we have cosmos from her garden. She's been there a year now, & is really good.

She's still so bashful that she practically crawls under her desk when anyone talks to her. It takes her two hours each way to come (& on trains jammed with Nips) & goes to night school to learn English. She makes ¥3,300 a month, about $12 at the present exchange. She dresses clean & neat, but her clothes are so old & worn. I gave her two dresses today that were too small for me—she really loved it & practically crawled under both our desks. When she recovered, she looked up "appreciate" in her Japanese-English dictionary, & after I helped her with a few pronunciations, she thanked me.

I had to laugh yesterday. They gave all our Japanese girls English exams, as the more they know the better pay they get. One little Jap. gal, who's been there just two weeks, went also. When they came back we asked her how she did. She's not too bright anyway & can't say anything but "Yes" in English. The Lt. said to her "Did you get 100%"? She gave him a big toothy grin & said "Yes". The other Japanese girls who understood him frantically tried to explain to her what he meant— guess they thought we might make her our interpreter—Annie (as she likes to be called) even seemed to have trouble understanding them. She still grinned & said "Yes" to every question.

Have been hearing 'bout the gas shortage in Calif. but didn't realize its gravity until you wrote.

Mom, would you please air mail a jar of "Mum" or "Arrid" or something like that? Darn PX hasn't had any for a long time, & my supply is getting critical. Got the best cheese, dates & magazines from Esther Bell last week. I was so glad to hear of your visit to Larry's. It seemed so long since I'd heard from him. I got a real nice letter from him too, last week.

Mom, I'm sure glad you went to have a check up, if you were not feeling well. How are the penicillin drugs working? Take life easy, kiddo, as I want my mamasan to always feel tops.

It's getting late; best I go to bed soon to be in shape for this weekend's trip.

Goodnight & all my love,
Norma Jean

21 Sept 1948

Dearest Esther & Dave,

Sure did enjoy that nice long newsy letter. Your visit with the Thomas' really sounded good. You certainly got around to lots of nice places.

Ooops—just had an interruption & have been laughing & laughing. Leonard from my office called; I thought he said it was Clarence. Since I know a Clarence I said, "Oh, Hello Clarence". He thought I said "Hello Clem". We've been going around & around getting Leonard, Clem & Clarence placed. I'll hear about this for a week at the office. By the way, did I ever tell you my office name? Ever since the song "Little Lulu" came out over here, they've been calling me "Little Lulu". War Dog, as we call Sgt. Cross, started it. He's about 50 years old & rather dignified. The first thing I knew someone was writing "Little Lulu" on my date pad every morning before I got to work. I'd get there & accuse all the G.I.'s of it & storm around while he just sat back & enjoyed it. Finally, I caught him one morning & was so surprised at him being the guilty one, that I was speechless. It's been "Little Lulu" ever since.

Your new deep freeze sounds wonderful. Do you have it yet? We've just been noticing all the recipes for deep freezing things in the magazines & saying how nice they are. The price sounds good too.

Emilie & I went to Ikaho last weekend. It's only about four hours from Tokyo in the mountains. It was sure cold. We had to take our own food, as it was a Japanese Hotel. I took the dates & cheese you sent. The dates were good as snacks on the train, & the cheese was luscious with our sukiyaki. We made our own version, which included rice, cheese, soy sauce, turkey (canned), fresh tomatoes, & fried onions. For dessert we had them cook some fresh apples we bought, added sugar & had more cheese with our applesauce.

Gad, I've been to a show since I finished the last paragraph. Am bound to finish this before the night's over though. We saw "Lady in Ermine" at the outdoor Tokyo Bowl. Pretty cute. The weather was just right outside.

Enjoyed the news of your luncheon at Lois' house. Golly, there have been so many changes since I left.

Am so mad at the PX. They don't have any opera glasses. I know they'll get more as soon as I buy something else for Faye. Nothing I've seen so far has been suitable & am hoping this weekend they'll have something.

Must close as it's late & time for bed.

Love,
Norma Jean

Nineteen

Dearest Esther & Dave,

It's a rainy Sunday morning, & everyone is either sleeping or reading, it seems. This is the beginning of Typhoon "Kit" we're told, so will probably have several rainy & windy days ahead of us. I've been studying those swell photography magazines you sent, Esther. Now, I'm all in the mood for some real "professional" picture taking, but no sun today. The boys at the bank got a look at them (especially the bathing suit pictures) & keep asking when they get a chance at "studying" my magazines.

I'd like to ask a favor of you Esther. Have been racking my brain what to get Emilie for Christmas. She's so hard to buy for as she has everything worthwhile having in Japan, & her Mother sends scads of everything. Anyhoo—after our trip to Korea we decided that Nylon lingerie would be the thing to have, as we were always waiting for things to dry—almost missed a train in Hakata 'cause our pants were still damp. So, I was wondering about getting her a pretty Nylon slip. I couldn't find any in the catalogs or magazines here, so I was wondering if you could. I will enclose $10. I don't know how much they are, but I'd like a nice one for her, & if there's much left over, or you can't get a slip, could you see about some other Nylon lingerie for her; she wears size 34. We may go to the Philippines in December, & I'd like her to have it for the trip, so could you send it within the next month?

You really must have had a scare with Dave's polio diagnosis. I hadn't heard about the big epidemic there.

Polio, or poliomyelitis, also known as Infantile Paralysis, was a worldwide scourge until vaccines were developed in the 1980's. The virus, which lives in the intestine and feces, was highly contagious. It rapidly affects the muscles, lungs, kidneys, and heart. When lungs were affected, patients were sometimes placed in cylinders dubbed "Iron Lungs" to assist breathing. There were about 2,000-3,000 cases in Japan in 1948 and about 4,200 cases in the U.S. In 1952, there were 58,000 cases in the U.S. Vaccinations reduced the worldwide incidence of polio from 350,000 cases in 1988 to 1,300 cases in 2007.

Sure enjoyed your snapshots. It's the first scene of the Bell's at home I've had.

Have been thinking of Mom a lot lately. She said in one of her letters she wasn't feeling too well, as you did too. Is she better? What did the Dr. say was wrong? With all of her activities, I could see why she'd be tired. Do you think working is too much for her?

Haven't been doing anything revolutionary lately. Saw "Oliver Twist" at the English Theatre & went to a Japanese nightclub last week. Have been invited to two sukiyaki dinners for the same night next week so am rather confused as to what to do about it. Bessie came back from Osaka—she's the one with relatives in Korea—so we've been talking about Korea. Lois wants us to come to dinner, so guess we'll be seeing her. She's all excited about her baby-to-be & is sewing little pink & blue things like a beaver. War Dog, Sgt. Cross, was called back into active duty & is now Capt. Cross. We're all so glad, as he's really nice & his wife is too. He's leaving the Bank though, so that leaves me to be right hand man of the Major—ugh!

Time for lunch & you know me. We'll have cold cuts, always do for Sunday lunch & chicken for dinner tonight.

All my love,
Norma Jean

7 October 1948

Dearest Mom & Dad,

It's Thursday evening & I just got home from work. Had a rough day at the Bank—everything seemed to go wrong. We can't make one account balance—it's off one gram.

Enjoyed your last letter so much. Haven't seen Lois yet but will give her the washing machine ad in the next couple of days. I was at her house last Sunday & had the best time. They called me up in the afternoon & said Gus, a friend of Bill's that I know, had bought 2 quarts of ice cream for the three of them & wanted me to come help them eat it. It was raining like everything, so Gus came & got me. They fed me ice cream, jellyrolls, popcorn & coffee while we listened to the USC-Ohio football game. I won $10 on the game from Gus—don't think he'll ever get over that afternoon. As soon as I got there Gus & Bill asked me to bet—they were both for Ohio & I said USC—with odds & points. They were so willing & both suggested 20 points. At the end of the third quarter with 10 to 1 odds, I knew something was wrong, as they both said the same thing & were so eager to get my dollar. Bill said he wouldn't bet but would hold the money. At the end of the third quarter the score was 13-0 & Gus was pulling his hair & just couldn't figure it out. Bill & Lois were practically laid out from laughing. It seems they had heard the score as 20-0 at the end of the 3rd quarter on a sports cast before the game was re-broadcast to us. The score was 20-0 in the very first part of the 4th quarter & the sports announcer said that. Poor Gus—$10 was all the money he had with him, & he had to go borrow, & hated to tell the fellows how he lost his money. He went back on guard & Lois, Bill & I went to see "Miranda" on Gus' money.

Haven't been doing much this week. It's been raining hard at times due to typhoons & then clears up & is sunny & warm. Okinawa was really hit hard by Typhoon "Libby." A friend of mine is in communications & had to take equipment to Okinawa night before last, as all of their equipment was down or broken.

Emilie & I are going to Karuiyana this weekend. Will stay at Allied Rest Hotel cottages & have our meals at the New Grand Lodge so won't have to take food with us.

Everyone is excited about them taking our 25% overseas differential next year. Am sure glad my contract will be up instead of just starting, if it really goes through. Must close & eat dinner.

All my love,
Norma Jean

17 October 1948

Dearest Mom & Dad,

It's Sunday morning. I've had breakfast, helped the room girl straighten the room, & am going to start getting ready to go to Lois' house for dinner shortly. She called last week & wanted to know if I liked Chow Mein as that's what she's having. We're having dinner about 12:30, then Bill, Lois, Gus (a friend of Bill's) & I are going to the football game, as the Cavalry are playing, & Bill & Gus never miss a Cav game.

Last night I went to a party & had the most luscious fried chicken. We didn't eat until nearly 9 o'clock, then they had piles of French fries & fried chicken. A friend of mine gave this party for a Captain & his wife who are going home. I laughed & laughed at our transportation. He decided we should have a bus as others said they had no way of getting there. I was picked up by the bus about 6:30. Two fellows & I went to pick the food up at the American Club then made our bus stops. Somehow, our bus route & time didn't agree with anyone else's, so the three of us had the whole bus to ourselves. It was a big bus marked "Special" & really seemed to confuse the other motorists. The others had gotten transportation & were waiting for us when we got there. My transportation has been unusual all week it seems. One night last week we were without a Jeep so had a rickshaw bring us home. It was fine until we had a flat tire—no one ever thought of a rickshaw getting a flat, but ours did, so we finally gave up & walked the rest of the way.

Your last letter was so good & newsy. Sure hope the oil strike ends soon. The shipping strike is the only one that affects us. Fresh eggs are getting mighty scarce & we have more canned foods. The shopping you did for me sounds good, am anxiously waiting for the package now.

Gee, it's time to go. Have to stop at the florist & get Lois a bouquet so must run. The dahlias are so pretty here now. We have a florist right in our hotel lobby so it's very handy.

Love,
Norma Jean

19 October 1948

Dearest Esther & Dave,

Have a guilty conscience as I received two of the most wonderful letters from you before answering & you're about 10 times busier than I am.

Have really enjoyed hearing about your deep freezer—it's really the thing. Will Mom be able to get one?

About the coffee sets, kiddo. Please don't send any money, as I don't know what it will be & anyhoo—I want to contribute something to the Bell household. I've been pricing tea & coffee sets for a long time & have bought one already. I'm waiting for the bargains I guess. Am just going to pick them up when I see them. The one I bought is a gorgeous demitasse set with 12 of the cutest & most fragile cups, saucers, coffee pot, sugar & creamer I've seen.

Am planning on getting more, then you & Mom can decide which you'd like, but I'm doing the same with pearls—have three strands now. I have different kinds, so we can trade around & wear ones best suited to our dresses. Back to the coffee sets—I bought the demitasse set at the little shop right here at the hotel, as they seem to have the best in town, so if Winnie wants one it would be no trouble, as they crate them & everything. I just don't know about the customs or breakage. About the scarf I sent; I never did find anything suitable for Faye. Think I'll send some more scarves to you, & if you think Faye would like one, I'd be pleased to give it to her. I'll send several—maybe Mom would like one also.

It's sure been getting cold here lately. The sky is so clear & blue, & we can see Fuji from our window in the morning & evening. It is snow-capped now.

Friday evening

I meant for this to be half way to California by now but was interrupted & just never got back on the beam.

Night before last, I was just going to start writing when the fire alarm sounded. I went out in the hall & talked it over with other gals & we decided best we go out. The lobby was filled with girls & when we asked, the man at the desk said two G.I.'s sounded the alarm by mistake. We came back to our rooms & were just settling down when the fire engines started to come. It had been a central alarm & fire engines from all over were rushing in.

Sunday morning

This is beginning to sound like a diary more than a letter. We've had another fire. The Bankers Club & the Red Cross center burned. It's just a block from us & everyone in the hotel behind us had to evacuate in case the fire spread. Practically everyone was there to watch—M.P.'s came by the truckload to keep the crowd under control. They got the fire out after the roof & second floor were burned out. It's the first large Allied building to burn in Tokyo since I've been here. No one was hurt.

I went to church this morning as the chief of all U.S. chaplains was there. It was packed, & the brass was there en masse.

We're going to see the movie "Hamlet" this afternoon. I heard that "Oliver Twist" was banned in the States. Is that true? I saw it here & it was very good.

The situation in Korea sounds quite critical. Emilie & I are so glad we went. Heaven only knows when American tourists will be allowed in again.

Must close for now & get ready to go to the show.

Love,
Norma Jean

29 October 1948

Dearest Mother & Dad,

I don't know how to begin. I called you this morning soon after I'd heard that terrible news of Emilie's death.

I'll start from the beginning of the week for all the details. We, Jack, Carl & I, went to see "Hamlet" at the Sunday matinee. Emilie & Mac had gone on a Jeep trip that morning. When I got home about six o'clock Emilie was in bed, & Hamako, our maid, was giving her a massage. I asked if she was feeling alright. She said she was tired but otherwise felt okay. She said she wasn't hungry & wouldn't let me have her dinner sent to the room. She wanted some coffee, so I brought her back a thermos of coffee. Emilie, Hamako, & I all had a cup of coffee together while she told me what a nice trip they had, & I told her how I liked the movie. The next morning, she said her back ached & thought she's stop in to see the Dr. When I came home at four-thirty, she was in bed again. She said the Dr. gave her some heat & light treatments & told her to come back the next day for an x-ray. She didn't eat any supper, & the maid was massaging her back. From seven to eight o'clock, I went to school, as Emilie said she was all right. The maid stayed with her until I came back. She said her back hurt, & her legs felt sore & she couldn't sleep. I had a sleeping pill the Dr. once gave me that I never used, so she said she'd like it. She took it & went right to sleep. In the morning, she said she had slept well, but her head ached, back ached, & she couldn't move her legs. She wasn't a bit frightened as she sincerely thought she had dislocated a vertebra on our trip to Korea, as she's been having back aches off & on since then. She thought a nerve had been pinched, which was causing her legs to be paralyzed. This was Tuesday morning. I ate breakfast & came back up to the room instead of going to work. I called her office & told them she wouldn't be in, then called her Dr. When I told him her symptoms he told me to call a Major (Dr.) in charge. Emilie was worried about my staying home. I didn't want to leave her, as she couldn't even get to the phone. She insisted, so Hamako & I pulled her bed over to the phone. She promised she'd call me when the Dr. came.

She called at my office about eleven o'clock & said she was going to the hospital for a little rest, as the Dr. had told her it might be a form of neuritis. I came home in about five minutes in order to pack things for her to take to the hospital. I waited with her for the ambulance. I helped her get on the stretcher & rode with her. She was quite weak, so I helped her answer entry questions & signed her deposit waiver. I helped them push the gurney up to isolation & said goodbye just outside the door. I waited & watched just where they put her, then came home.

We had made out a little system of communication & settled details like mail, calling her office, etc. I went out that night but of course couldn't see her. The next day, our system was supposed to work, but it didn't. I was practically frantic by the time I got home from work, so called the hospital. I insisted on talking to her Dr. He was very nice, but when he told me she had polio, I just gasped. He wanted me to call again after he made the rounds. I gave a message for him to give Emilie, & when I called him he gave me a message from Emilie, so I knew she was conscious.

The next morning, I went to my Dr. & told him everything & asked what I should do about fumigating, what could, & was being done for Emilie, etc. He was very nice & helpful. He said nothing could be done about prevention & called the hospital & said Emilie was in an iron lung but holding her own. He gave me a blood count the results of which showed just a little anemic, so he gave me iron pills.

I went to the hospital & took her some slippers that she's been wanting. The next morning, I talked to the nurse, & she said Emilie wanted me to know she got the slippers & liked them, so I knew she was still conscious. Last night, I went out, then called. All they'd tell me was she was resting well. I was so worried all night.

I went to work this morning, & about nine o'clock a Lt. Col. & Maj. from her office came in & told me she had died at 8:25. They had been out there & seen the Dr. I was so glad they came instead of letting the hospital call me. The Lt. Col. & I went to the Club & talked & decided what to do. I just had to talk to you, so we went over & got the call through without any waiting.

We had lunch, then I came home. Pretty soon the Chaplain called, & I said I'd like to see him. He was very nice & stayed with me almost all afternoon. We decided it would be nice to have a Memorial Service for Emilie. I told him Emilie & I always liked Chapel Center best, so we're having it there probably next Wednesday. We agreed perfectly on the type of service we thought Emilie would have wanted. I'm getting a friend of Emilie's & mine to play the organ, & I'm notifying friends. A medical officer came also & wants to air the room for twelve hours.[33] The manager was up & asked if I'd like another room. I told him I want to stay right here as I'm getting important calls & want to stay with her things to be sure they're taken care of properly. He said he'd give me a room close for one night while they aired it. They want me to go through Emilie's personal letters & take out things, which might be hard on her Mother. Also, a lady from the hotel, someone from Emilie's section, & I will inventory all of her things & get them ready for packing.

That's everything so far. I'm feeling fine. Have no appetite, but people are so nice about seeing I have regular & good meals that I haven't missed a meal. I don't know what I'll do. All I want right now is to finish the details & come home. If I decide to I'll let you know. I can come for forty-five days leave or come home for good. I'll not do anything until I have thought it all out. The Chaplain & I talked about letters to Grafs. He will write, & I will. I want to call them also. He was with Emilie in the hospital & told me everything. She was paralyzed terribly—all over. She was tremendously brave & never gave up. When they put her in the iron lung instead of being frightened she said, "This is interesting." He said not until last night about 10 o'clock, did she seem the least bit anxious. Then breathing became so difficult. A Col. (the head of the Dr's. here), nurse & chaplain were with her all night & until she died this morning.

They brought me a package from the office this afternoon. It was the gloves & bag. They're gorgeous—will wear them for Emilie's service. Tell Esther I got the slip she bought for me to give Emilie. It's lovely.

I feel so much better after having called you & talking with the chaplain. I've decided I'll do everything possible for Emilie & her parents. I feel the best tribute to her will be helping in any way I can, living a normal & healthy life with beautiful & pleasant memories of her.

---

33 In 1948, it was not known exactly how polio was spread. Jean was probably not in any danger of contracting the disease, because she, her sister, brother & mother all simultaneously had polio in 1927 while they were moving from Washington State to California.

Must close for now as the phone keeps ringing & girls drop in, as people just can't comprehend it's really true.

All my love to my wonderful family. Thanks Mom & Dad for being so nice on the phone—I hardly knew what I was saying. Give my love to Esther & Larry.

Love,
Norma Jean

Mrs. Arnold U. Graf
Route 1
Vashon Island, Washington
I can't locate her home phone number as yet.

Mr. Arnold U. Graf
1110 3rd Avenue
Seattle, Washington

Twenty

4 November 1948

Dearest Family,

This is the first day since the tragic news of Emilie that I've felt up to writing or anything else. Guess it's because I think I'll soon be seeing you. It's not for sure yet, but here's the dope. Eighth Army said I could take my leave in the States. The ships are very crowded now, as many are going home for Christmas. The Personnel Office said that under my circumstances, they'd make a special effort to get me a booking the last of November or 1st of December. They pay my fare both ways—I only have to pay from the port of debarkation to my home. I will take a 45 day leave as that's what they give for Stateside leaves. I have about 30 days coming with pay, so will lose only about 15 days pay. I will not have to sign another contract so can stay whatever time I want when I return. Another thing that persuaded me—after the first of the year our 25% overseas differential will stop—we'll probably get some living allowance. Anyway—I'll be losing money on leave if I don't take it before the first of the year. That's why Emilie & I were taking our vacation in December. I'll let you in on the developments. My office said I could go, so will start the red tape. Gosh, I don't know if it's the right thing or not but have a feeling it is. I talked to Mr. Graf over the phone Tuesday, & he said they'd like to see me, so I will be able to see them in Seattle. Anything I could do to relieve any anxiety they may have would be worth working months for. He was so nice to talk with.

Mrs. Graf did not talk, probably wasn't able. Their big worry was to know if Emilie had been alone. I assured them I was with her as long as possible & that she had the best of care in the hospital day & night. I also wrote them a letter & am telegraphing flowers.

Golly, I've never had so many difficult decisions to make. The Chaplain was wonderful & helped me with details. We had the Memorial Service yesterday. I told him I didn't want anything morbid or any sad songs, as Emilie & I had talked about those things. We got the best organist available, & he played lots of lovely music, the chaplain gave a scripture lesson, the twenty-fourth Psalm, a few words on Emilie's courage & vitality for life, we sang "Sweet Hour of Prayer" & "Be Still My Soul", then the benediction. Everyone I spoke with said they thought it was fitting & inspirational, & I was so glad there was not a lot of crying & emotion. The Dr. gave me some nerve pills, & it was much easier than I thought it would be. One of the last things Emilie said was, she was glad the ambulance was a little late & didn't get here at lunch time when all the girls would be home. She said "I don't want to be dramatic".

I've stayed home from work all week partly because I felt so lousy, & I had to help them inventory all of Emilie's things. She has piles & piles. We've been inventorying & packing for three days now, & we still have loads to do. I'm watching & giving the Captain a bad time whenever he doesn't pack things the way I think they should be done. He's really doing a good job though. The worst thing was to choose the clothes to take to the undertaker. I just pray my decisions are right. Tokyo was just shocked at Emilie's death, & everyone has been so nice to me. The only unpleasant thing I'm having to face now are the rumors. I hate gossip & rumors & a few have gotten back to me, which makes it very difficult. For example, one rumor was that she died right in our room. I feel that if I get away, I will avoid much of this. I really love it here & want to come back, as it's something really worthwhile, & I've met so many really nice people, & have many friends here now. Gee, I bet this sounds confusing to you—but I'm confused too. It would be nice if someone would just tell me what to do but realize that unless I make these decisions myself, I would not be satisfied.

I received your letter today, Mom, thanks. It was so nice & newsy. Also received the shoes, hat, & food (Esther sent the goodies--oh, so good!). I'm just wild about the shoes & hat. The shoes fit perfectly, & I like the hat style.

Must close & get to the Bank before the inventory boys arrive. Thank you for everything. I'm so proud of my family.

Love,
Norma Jean

9 November 1948

Dearest Family,

I received your letter yesterday, Mom—the one you wrote after talking to me on the phone. Since I last wrote, many things have happened. I had it all set to come home right away, then come back again on an indefinite contract—which would mean they'd pay my way every trip & the most I'd have to come back for would be three months. We had so many things planned for this spring, & it's hard to leave those things undone. But, the Communists have changed everything. Yesterday, Eighth Army called & said all ships have been re-routed to China to evacuate American dependants—so no ships for Japan until January they think.[34] This means I'll complete my contract on January 7 & will get the first available ship—Eighth Army is giving me some priority over others due to circumstances—otherwise, it may be months before I could get on the list. Gad, what a life. After yesterday, I decided not to even try anymore. Am not going to worry about anything, because it's useless anyway. Will just get on the ship when they tell me, whether it's one month, or six months from now, & not think about it until then.

---

34 Americans were being evacuated to Japan, the Philippines, and the United States as the Communists were winning their battles against the Nationalists. The take-over by the Communists was complete by 1950.

I got a very sad letter from Mrs. Graf yesterday. It just made me sick to read it. The big thing that's been bothering me is that Emilie's body is still here, & with this shipping problem they can't tell me when it will go home. I've talked with Capt. Cox, the officer appointed her executor, & a Col., about it, to see if there wasn't someway to cut the red tape, but so far have gotten nowhere.

Emilie's things are still in the room with me. They've been inventoried & partly packed, which leaves the room looking like a warehouse. Capt. Cox & a crew from shipping & crating section are coming this afternoon, they say to clean things up—which I doubt very much. I'm staying at home when they come to see they get everything of hers & nothing of mine.

It's a beautiful day in Tokyo, & I have so much to do. Have been going to work every day, but am just gold bricking this morning, because I know I can get away with it—official time due to Capt. Cox coming. Must close & whip over to the Bank & PX.

Love,
Norma Jean

10 November 1948

Dearest Sister,

I received your nice letter & magazines & package today. The Nylon undies are lovely. You always have the loveliest thoughts of what I'd like. Shipping is all tied up over here now, so I just don't know when I'll be able to make a booking. They're very nice to me, & I'm so glad I asked right away, for I will get the first space available; for one with my priority—probably in January, they say. If I'd waited, it would have been longer. It just depends on the China crisis & emergency listings ahead of me. I'm taking very good care of myself, so don't worry. I lost a little weight but the Dr. is giving me extra iron & vitamins, & he said I was perfectly all right. When I get very tired or tense at the office, I just come home & rest—usually I feel disgusted with the Army & am afraid I'll tell them so, which wouldn't help matters at all. They've been awfully nice though & give me all the time I want without counting it against either my annual leave or sick leave.

I received another letter from Mrs. Graf today. It was not quite as pathetic as yesterday's but my heart just aches when I read them. I feel so utterly helpless but think I can help them in many ways by taking care of details here. We inventoried & packed for five days, & just yesterday the shipping & crating Lt. came & took the things from our room. I'm working on the Army to cut as much red tape as possible, but it's about futile. A Col. from her section is helping lots.

Esther darling, the best thing you could do for me is take care of yourself & not worry. I'm all right & my many good friends in Tokyo are just wonderful to me. My goodness, my two little maids won't even let me comb my own hair anymore if they're around. They started crying all over again when I said I may be going home—I felt so sorry for them. They keep my room filled with beautiful bouquets of chrysanthemums. It's so funny; they've doubled their attack on washing & ironing practically have my P.J.'s in the suds before I have them off. Bet I'm the cleanest kid in Tokyo!

Golly, kiddo, think I'd talk 72 hrs. straight, if you were here right now. We'll catch up soon. I'm so glad I'm here right now to help the Graf's.

Must close & write to Mrs. Graf & some of Emilie's friends. Tomorrow is a holiday, Armistice Day. Am just going to take it easy. It's lovely fall weather now & is so invigorating.

Thanks again for everything. Give my love to Dave.

Love,
Norma Jean

13 November 1948

Dearest Mom & Dad,

I can't tell you how happy I was to receive those wonderful letters from you both on Friday. Have felt much better ever since. I don't feel so utterly confused & am getting the old spirit back on things I want to do. Now, my plans are to come home in January—the Communists willing. If I can get a job that pays a whole lot, I may come back for a few months just for the money, but so far nothing sounds good enough. Tokyo is feeling the effects of the American citizens leaving China. So far, two of the women's hotels are preparing to take them in, & our hotel will be next if needed. It's really rough on shipping out of Japan though, as all ships are being held in abeyance if they're not going to China. It's rather exciting—gee, I'd hate to have missed this. The gals are moaning & groaning because they have to move or double up. We're in no danger at all here but feel close to the changing world situation.

Friday was an important day in Japan's history with the verdict of the war criminals being given. The Nips were clustered around radios all over the city listening to the results. Most American officers had radios, too. Japanese extras came out in the afternoon & the little newsmen were ringing bells, yelling & running down the streets. The sentences given seemed to be about what everyone expected.[35]

We're supposed to mail our Christmas packages home by November 15th. Everyone has been wrapping madly. Jack & Carl were wrapping theirs. When they finished, Jack had wrapped a pair of scissors in his, & Carl had included his good pen, so they had to unwrap everything to find them. Our office looked like the wrapping section in a department store Friday afternoon. Some of the wives came down to do some last minute things. I just haven't been able to get any spirit for it. Would it be all right if I just sent you some money this year? I have gifts for everyone but the customs is high for anything of value, & I really expect to be home before too long. I probably won't have any customs to pay as we're allowed $500 a year customs free. I would like to send some money—maybe I could help with your Christmas turkey

---

35 Seven men received death sentences, 16 defendants were sentenced to life imprisonment, and two received prison terms. Two defendants died during the trials, and one was set free due to an insanity ruling.

or something you wanted. I'm having a terrific time trying to think of something to send the Grafs. Emilie has boxes & boxes of souvenirs & lovely things from Japan that they will get so I'm really puzzled. Do you think a flowering plant or flowers would be suitable? I can arrange that through florists from here. Golly, I just don't know.

Sunday Morning—

It's a beautiful, beautiful morning in Tokyo. It's sunny, clear blue skies & that lovely fall air. I could see Fuji when I looked out my window this morning. The Palace moat across the street looks positively picturesque. Am going shopping on the Ginza—a surprise gift for one of you that I've been thinking about—but you have to wait 'til I get there. This afternoon "our boys" from the Bank are playing football, & I'm supposed to go & cheer them on.

Can't wait to get out in the sunshine, so will close for now.

All my love,
Norma Jean

15 November 1948

Dearest folks,

Just a tiny note while I'm waiting for my dinner date. Received your nice letter today, Mom. I surely appreciate your writing often—mail call is the most important thing in my day.

Was so glad to hear of your phone call to the Grafs. I was so excited when I read that they can come to California. Gee, I'm so lucky to have such a wonderful family!

Nothing new as far as my plans go. A Major with whom I used to work at the Bank called from Hokkaido, the northern island, & asked about my working there. I told him that unless I'd be getting a good raise I was not interested. He couldn't promise, so I think it's out. It's fun being a brat—my little wheels are grinding, & I have lots of ideas what I want to do—that is, after I have had as much time with you as I want.

My little Japanese typist brought me a "presento" today for when I go to America. It's a gorgeous lacquer candy dish. I think the nicest part of Japan is the women.

Time for that dinner, & I'm starved-our food is sure tiresome now, due to the shipping strike.[36] Will eat you out of house & home when I get there.

Love xxx OOO
N.J.

16 November 1948

Dearest Esther & Dave,

Just got home from the Bank & have half an hour to wait before dinner time. Right now I'm thinking longingly of those luscious steaks from your freezer. Our food is strictly lousy now because of the shipping strike. No fresh vegetables, fruits, or milk. The American Club used to serve luscious stateside food, but they ran out, too. Went to the Imperial Hotel for lunch today with some news correspondent friends. Cols. & above are billeted there & they usually have the best food, but it was just the same as ours today. Am really not complaining but just warning you about my appetite for stateside food—especially from freezers!

Would love to see your "new look" hairstyle. Isn't Mom wonderful in being able to always help us with everything?

It's been raining all day today & is quite cold. I bought a new black gabardine raincoat with a detachable hood & am really enjoying it now. My red boots from last year look real flashy with it.

I don't have a roommate. The Army & Hotel asked if I wanted to move, but that would be awful to have to move all my things. People

---

36 This refers to the strike by the International Longshoremen's & Warehousemen's Union (ILWU) which tied up shipping from West Coast ports.

wouldn't know where I was, & I wanted to be right here in case of important messages.

Thursday, Nov. 18

Here I go again. Someday, I'll finish a letter on the same day I started it.

Yesterday, I got the "Life" you sent & have really enjoyed it. The article on U.C. & UCLA were especially good.

Haven't been doing much lately. I saw "No Minor Vices"—real funny & cute. Bessie & I are thinking about going to Karuizawa in the mountains this weekend. She's so good to me & thinks the change & mountain air is just what I need. Will get a chance to wear those beautiful birthday undies you sent.

Haven't heard any more on available shipping space. News from China doesn't sound very encouraging—more evacuations being planned. Can't wait to tell about what I'm getting for you. The little man downstairs promised to pick out a real pretty tea set—it will be here next week.

Goodnight for now,
Love, Norma Jean

November 17, 1948

Dear Miss Jean,

The sudden death of Miss Emilie was such a great shock to me, & I can hardly believe that she is no more in this world; it is like a dream. I have been feeling very lonely, so you must have felt it still more. When she was alive, she was so nice to me, giving me many kindnesses whenever I was in trouble. That sympathetic & hearty kindness never would I forget throughout my life.

I am also very thankful for the various nice things you have given me as her keepsake. Thank you for your consideration. I shall not fail to keep them carefully as long as they last.

As I can't write English, I asked one of my acquaintances to write to you on my behalf, but I am sure it is beyond description, how I miss Miss Emilie & how I've been thankful for you being thoughtful of me.

Yours sincerely[37]

21 November 1948

Dearest Mom & Dad,

Bessie & I are spending Saturday, Sunday, & Monday in Karuizawa. It is in the mountains & is very cold. Friday, we had a slight typhoon. It was gorgeous Saturday coming up here, & the rain & wind had left everything looking so green & clean. The sun is very bright, & the air so brisk & clear. Bessie is so good to me. She is of Korean ancestry & her home is in Hawaii. She knew Emilie very well & is so understanding. We went bicycling & shopping today. We found a little wood carving factory & each ordered two small chests with drawers. We've been planning on how we're going to fix our stateside rooms a'la oriental. Being Oriental herself she has some wonderful ideas. Gad, at this rate I'll need a truck to get my stuff home in from the stations. It's loads of fun though. Right now we're sitting in front of a roaring fire in the fireplace, eating peanuts, writing & reading. Tomorrow, we're planning on taking a walk to Sunset Point, then catching the afternoon train for Tokyo. We spent all our yen so can't do anymore shopping—our favorite recreation.

Thursday will be our Thanksgiving holiday. A special shipment was made, so we can have turkey with all the trimmings for Thanksgiving & Christmas. Have been invited to dinner with Jack & Carl, so we three will celebrate together. I became acquainted with them through John Hawes. Do you remember John? He, Emilie & I were always going places together. John is somewhere in China now. I surely would like to have him know about Emilie, but it's impossible to contact him. I

---

37 This note was not signed, but it was probably from one of the maids.

wrote to his parents in the hope they will know of some forwarding address. The last I heard, he was somewhere in the interior of China waiting for a convoy to get out. He is flying from there over the hump into India, where he'll spend some time. From there he may come back to Japan & go home or go home via Africa. His brother & he went together into China. His brother is planning on spending three years near Chunking teaching English in a university. He got the job through a scholarship at Oberlin College. Really an interesting family, & I sure hope they come out all right in the present crisis.

I received another letter from Mrs. Graf Friday & have just finished writing to her. Lt. Col. Lockett & I are getting together again next week & will try to find out a definite answer on a shipping date for Emilie's body, as the Grafs, naturally, are very concerned about this.

Bessie & I are sitting here planning an evening for next week. So far we've decided to eat at the Union Jack Club, the Australian Club, then go see a Korean opera at a Japanese theatre.

One shipload of American evacuees from China was due here yesterday, & we are anxious to see if our hotels will be affected when we get back. Never a dull moment.

The fire is making me sleepy, so think I'll take a hot bath & go to bed. Goodnight.

All my love,
Norma Jean

23 November 1948

Dearest Momasan & Papasan,

What a lovely surprise I had today! A package from "310" with the nicest birthday presents & card. I just love the blouse—it fits just right, & the color is gorgeous. Am munching on the chocolate covered cherries—do they ever hit the spot. The PX candy is so stale, due to the shipping hold up, & this tastes so fresh & good. The card is really beautiful & looks cute on my dressing table. Thanks loads & loads for everything. I'll wear my blouse for Thanksgiving.

I got back to Tokyo about 9:30 last night. We hated to leave that good food & invigorating mountain air. The town is full of Naval personnel, as a task force landed while we were away. The dependants from China arrived also. I heard this morning that the management at the Osaka Hotel in Tokyo (a women's hotel) was chagrined when a 20-year-old boy came to live at the hotel. He was a dependant & guess they didn't notice his age.

Work at the Bank is so boring now. I'm not busy unless things are coming in or leaving the vaults, & nothing's been happening at all. I've got to scrounge work for the others & put up a front myself, which makes it very monotonous. I get so disgusted with Civil Service & the Army at times, as lack of good management & organization along with personal prejudices are so evident. But it has its advantages, too. Maybe I'm just spoiled from too many holidays.

Jack just called & said we are going to two Thanksgiving dinners. One at his hotel at noon & one at the American Club in the evening. I'll probably have turkey out the ears by the time this day is over. I'll be thinking of you, especially that day & do hope you have a nice holiday.

Thanks again for my birthday gifts—am sure glad I decided to come to your house.

All my love,
Norma Jean

P.S. There are some pictures Larry sent me & wanted me to forward to you. He's really a "good guy."

Twenty-one

1 December 1948

Dearest Mom & Dad,

It seems as though it's been quite a while since I've written—I'm sorry. Have been very busy & have been so tired. Am taking it easy this week to make up for it.

Had a lovely Thanksgiving—gad—never ate two such huge turkey dinners in the same day.

This evening, when I came in, a girl, Mary Ford, was in the room. She's older than I & seems quite nice. Nothing seems right here anymore, & I dreaded having to get adjusted to living with someone else. It's probably a good thing for me though.

I talked with 8th Army Saturday about my departure date. They said I could not go before February. I was hoping they'd say January, but no luck. I found out one good thing though. Since I signed my contract in New York, I will get money to cover travel expenses to N.Y. It will probably be around $100, which will be a useful item with stateside prices.

I finally found out when they expect to ship Emilie's body. She's supposed to leave the 4th of December on the Gen'l Ainsworth. I'm just praying that everything works out, as the Graf's are just desperate. She has been ill. Sunday I went to church where Chaplain Anderson, the one who was with Emilie at the hospital, conducts the service. He & his wife & I had a nice visit afterward. I told you didn't I that they had me visit them all afternoon & evening the Sunday after Emilie died? They have a darling little boy a year & a half old. They certainly have been a wonderful help.

I received a very nice letter from John Hawes' mother. She thinks he's in India now & is forwarding my letter on.

We're having our office Christmas party this Saturday, Dec. 4th. It seems so early for a Christmas party, but some of those characters thought they were so popular in the Christmas season that they couldn't come if it were later. Our Col. insisted that we have rice, wieners & sauerkraut with our turkey. It seems a little revolting to us, but knowing him, it's typical. We decided to set a few packages of "Tums" by the sauerkraut.

Is it ever getting cold. That birthday blouse is just wonderful to wear in the evenings—so nice & warm yet so good looking. Since I'm going to be here a while, maybe I'll get to go skiing once again. Think I'll take a little vacation if I can get in an Allied ski hotel. Just love vacations!

Hate to cut this short but am so tired & in a low mood so will write more & pleasanter soon. Please take good care of yourselves.

All my love,
Norma Jean

3 December 1948

Dearest Mom & Dad,

Just a note before dinner. Am feeling in a much lighter mood than the last time I wrote & not tired. The Dr. had me come back for another blood count. I got the results yesterday, & he said it was normal, & I wouldn't have to take any more iron or vitamin pills— which really helped my morale too. Have been resting lots & told my friends this is my "Be Kind to Jean Week".

I received two letters from you today, Mom, & surely did enjoy them. That was so nice of Esther Heylen to send Jean Stier's wedding picture & announcement. I was so sorry to hear of Aunt Lou's illness. I will be sure & send her a Christmas card.

Esther & Dave are surely doing well & have so many nice things. I'm so happy for them. I get so excited when I think of seeing them & their home & cars. I really chuckled when you told about cleaning house when you thought I'd be coming home. Don't knock yourselves out—310 would look good to me if it were covered with a foot of dust. Anyhoo—I'll want to try out that new vacuum cleaner.

Saturday

Just got home from our office Christmas party. It was really very nice. About 70 people were there. We had three turkeys, ham, potatoes, giblet gravy, cranberry sauce, Jello salad, rolls, olives, rice & chocolate sundaes with cookies. Our Col. made a speech & the President of the Bank did too. The Nips entertained by singing, & then we sang for them. Don't know what happened to the Col's wieners & sauerkraut but was sure relieved not to see them. Our six little typists came dressed in their prettiest kimonos & really looked pretty & colorful.

Jack just called—the fourth time in two hours. He's nice & has done so many nice things for me, but he's getting to be a problem as he's so serious. Now he wants to go home the same time I'm going. Me & my problems.

Emilie was supposed to go home on the Gen'l Ainsworth which sailed today. I'm terribly afraid it didn't work out as Captain Cox said he'd call me this morning to tell me, & he never called. If she didn't, I just dread writing the Grafs again. Col. Lockett said if she didn't, he'd try to see why not & write to them also. He's been very helpful. We have dinner together once in a while & get things straightened out as much as possible.

We had a lot of flowers at our party today, & all of the ladies were given bouquets when we left. Mine looks so pretty on my dresser. The Japanese Bank President invited us all to a Christmas party they are giving for us in return. Guess the holiday festivities have officially started in Tokyo. It will be a mad race until after New Years now.

The PX is decorated & really looks nice. Sure wish you could join me in a shopping tour as they have some gorgeous oriental things for sale—rugs, pianos, jewelry, silk & oodles of souvenirs. They're having a big drive to help the orphanages in Tokyo. Before, nothing like that was allowed. The policies of the occupation are changing.

Tomorrow, Bessie & I are going to visit Capt. & Mrs. Cross (War Dog). Am going to start sending Christmas cards too but hate to think of all the letters I should enclose. Guess I'll get started on a few tonight.

It's been nice visiting with you tonight. Goodnight, my dears.

Love,

N. J. jr

P.S. Just heard about the earthquake in California. Everything under control?

10 December 1948

Dearest Mom & Dad,

Just had to add a note with the card. Have been very busy this week it seems, & my "Christmas carding" has gotten ahead of me.

Am enclosing a $25 money order. Hope you can use it in your Christmas celebrating. Will Larry be able to be home? I will sure be thinking of you especially hard on Christmas. It would be nice if I could have made it home by then—but, gee, I'll have two big holidays this way—Christmas in Tokyo & Homecoming Day in Compton.

I've gotten lots of invitations to visit my friends' homes before Christmas & on Christmas Day; Jack & I will eat one of those luscious American Club, super holiday meals.

I took the morning off to go to Yokohama to see Bessie off on her way home for a vacation. I hated to have her leave, but when I saw how excited & truly happy she was today, I was so happy for her too. She had a lovely stateroom on a nice ship & will be home for Christmas. Helen & I caught the 6:47 a.m. train for Yokohama. We went aboard & Bessie gave us a tour of the ship. The band was there & played as the ship pulled away. It's going to Guam, Hawaii & California, so they played "California Here I Come" & "Aloha Oe" as two of their selections. There were a lot of Japanese war brides aboard & many Japanese families ashore to see them leave. Anyone who says the Nips aren't emotional should have been there—Japanese men, women & children aboard & ashore were crying. Bessie heard on my birthday that she was going, so we celebrated together that night. She was called at 2 in the afternoon & by 4 o'clock had her things at the warehouse to be crated & put aboard. She has hardly slept since then from excitement.

Well, dearies, must close for now & do a little more "carding" before I go to bed. No, think I'll go right to bed—these early morning train rides don't agree with me. Goodnight for now.

Merry Christmas & have a real good time.

All my love,
Norma Jean

14 December 1948

Dearest Family,

I got the most interesting looking packages in yesterday's mail. Can hardly wait until December 25th! They sure are tempting.

Tomorrow is going to be a busy day, so have been getting ready for it tonight. Right after work I'm supposed to go to a meeting of some Japanese in the Bank & give a speech. They've asked me several times, but I never got there. Yesterday, two men very formally came in & said this was the last meeting of the year & invited me to be their guest & speaker. Since they can hardly understand English, I decided the speech wouldn't be difficult, so I accepted. After that I'm going to a formal dinner-dance at the American Club, so I've been organizing my wardrobe for that. I have just had a fuchsia brocade evening blouse made which I'll wear with my black evening skirt, long black gloves, gold sandals, & gold evening bag. Then Thursday, in school, Friday dinner with Col. Lockett, then the weekend—think I'll just rest Saturday & Sunday. Time sure goes fast.

Must finish the notes for tomorrow's speech, so best I get to work. Don't know how I get into such things. Goodnight for now. If you see Santa be sure & thank him for the things he brought me.

Love, Norma Jean

20 December 1948

Dearest Mom & Dad,

It's Sunday morning & so quiet & peaceful. Have just finished breakfast & am waiting for Michi to come, as we are going to visit some Japanese friends this morning. After that I must go to the PX to get a few Christmas gifts. From 5 to 7, I am going to an open house affair, & then at 7:30, Jack & I are going to see the "Messiah". Yesterday, I went on a trip about two hours out of Tokyo to see Hirohito's grandfather's tomb. It was a beautiful day & the mountainous countryside was so pretty. Had a nice time & was back in Tokyo around 5 o'clock.

I got a letter from John Hawes last week. I was sure glad to know he had gotten mine in India. He wrote from Lahore, Pakistan, India. He was leaving there in a few days for Paris, France. I was supposed to write him there, but his letter took nearly a month from India, & he would have already left Paris by the time my letter would get there. He expects to be home in the middle of January. What a wonderful trip he's had, & he's just the type to get so much out of it.

Have been getting so many nice letters & cards from the States. Would like to write each one a long letter, but there just doesn't seem to be enough hours in the day to get everything done. I received another lovely letter from Mrs. Graf. She asked about some business affairs of Emilie's, which I found out about & answered immediately. She said they were planning on going to California after the first of the year. I was so glad to hear her planning this, as I know she must be feeling well enough to undertake it. Emilie's body should have gotten there this weekend, & I certainly have been thinking of her folks. Her office sent a cable ordering a large flower arrangement to be sent to her parents. I thought that was nice of them.

Next week, we get Thursday afternoon off to see a Christmas parade & Friday afternoon off. Friday morning, we're having another little party at the office. We'll give little gifts to our Japanese help then. Oh, yes, my speech at the Japanese Club meeting turned out very well—it was really a riot, & I had lots of fun. I surely wasn't nervous about talking, because only one person could understand a word I was saying. What an audience—they (about 30) sat there so attentively trying to catch a familiar word, then all clapped madly when I had finished. They all asked questions about America when I finished, & it was a scream. They have the most fantastic ideas of what goes on over there. They wanted to know all about Santa Claus, so I told them the story (in basic English). They also wanted to know if American women smoked cigars, have matched marriages & what the go-between's were doing in the States, why didn't I become a movie star because they thought anyone could if they wanted, Stateside, & all sorts of other questions. We had tea, fruit & candy to eat. They gave me a cute little doll as a present, & about three members invited me to their homes—which I refused tactfully.

The formal dance I went to later that same night was really lovely. The Club looked out-of-this-world. It's really elegant. It's called the Rose Room, & they had huge bouquets of roses all around & a rose corsage on every table. The upholstery & rugs are all rose or deep red & the gorgeous chandeliers had blue lights in them. I was pleased with my formal, & everyone seemed to like it, so my evening was really a happy one.

I'm anxious to hear how your Christmas was. Hope everything was fine, as I know it will be. Did you have a tree? This will probably get there after Christmas, which is hard to believe. I'm going to have lots of fun Christmas, but really I'm saving my gayest spirit for my California holiday. Ooops—here's Michi "Sayonara" & lots & lots of love.

Norma Jean

26 December 1948

Dearest Esther & Dave,

Thank you for making my Christmas in Tokyo such a good one. Your letters & cards were so lovely, & the gold belt & perfume made me practically squeal with delight. Have really been needing a gold belt, & it goes so well with the gold sequin bag Mom sent. The perfume will be perfect for my travel, as I have no suitable traveling perfume, & Aphrodesia is my very favorite. The packages were wrapped so cute; I had a gay time opening them. The food sure tastes good, too.

It seems impossible that you will have been married for nearly a year. It seems very natural for me to be writing to Mr. & Mrs. Bell, however, but will probably really appreciate the changes when I can see you in your own little home. Bet your house looked cute with all its Christmas decorations.

I really had a nice Christmas. Have been busy every minute. This is the first evening I've been home for over a week & I'm really enjoying a quiet, rainy evening. I slept almost all morning & feel so relaxed & lazy tonight. The overseas radio Christmas-special program is going to be on shortly, so I will listen to that. Thank you for everything. Goodnight for now.

All my love,
Norma Jean

26 December 1948

Dearest Mom & Dad,

It's the day after Christmas, & Tokyo is really quiet. It's raining, & everyone I know is staying home & sleeping & recuperating. I really had a nice time. When Christmas Eve came, I could contain my curiosity no longer & opened my packages with Mary. Thanks loads for everything. I've been eating those delicious dried fruits & nuts all afternoon, & they sure are good. Just love that gold sequin bag, Mom. So many of the girls have them & take them to the clubs—with or without formals, so it will

227

surely be useful. Think I'll initiate it New Years Eve. The slippers are darling & so comfy. They'll be nice for traveling too, as they're nice & flat. The marshmallows, fruitcake & dates really are good—just had to sample them. I imagine you saw the gorgeous gold belt & Aphrodesia perfume Esther & Dave gave me. It was so nice. I also got a pretty blouse from Clarice, a scarf, handkerchief case, gold pin, photo book, Japanese dolls, & flowers. The tissues you sent sure came in handy—we gave our little maids a party & used the tissues for napkins. We had fun & fixed fish, cheese, & turkey sandwiches, with orange juice, cookies, candy, nuts & the dried fruit. They really liked it. We also gave them some little gifts—I gave cosmetics & Mary gave them stockings. This is the first time I've been home for the day in a long time it seems. I've been visiting friends all week & went to two open houses yesterday. Christmas Eve, Jack & I went to see the stage show at the Ernie Pyle & then to the American Club. Last night, we went to the Dinner-Dance at the Club, which was really elaborate. It was all fun, but I'm rather glad it's over too. Our Col. gave us each a day off, so I'm taking next Thursday off. New Years Eve, Jack & I are going to a party, then New Years Day the Lt. Col. & Major in my office are each having open houses, which we're supposed to attend. Also, one of the little maids has invited me to her house, which should be interesting.

Am anxious to hear about your Christmas. Sure thought about you, but your plans sounded good, so I knew you'd be having fun.

I've never heard Christmas carols so much before as this year. The bus terminal is right across the street from our Hotel, & they played Christmas carols over the public address system for three days from 8 a.m. to 11 p.m. Christmas morning they turned it up real loud & woke everyone who might be sleeping at 8 o'clock with these songs.

My replacement is supposed to arrive at the Bank shortly. It will really seem certain that I'm going when I start training her. Haven't heard anything from the Grafs for a while but imagine they've been terribly busy & upset.

Must close & wash my hair, for tomorrow is another working day. Goodnight my dears, & thank you so much for the nice Christmas presents. You always seem to know just what I like.

All my love,
Norma Jean

P.S. Monday a.m. Just had mail call, I got 22 letters & cards this morning. The Kansas kin were so nice—letters & cards from all of them. Am enjoying two letters from "310". Tell Ruby Bird I received her friendly letter & card—it was so cute of her to remember me.

28 December 1948

Dearest Esther & Dave,

Just a tiny letter tonight. Just remembered that I would like some more color film before I leave & wondered if you'd be so kind as to get it for me. I forgot how much it is, but if $5 is enough for 1 roll of 35 mm Kodachrome & 1 roll of 35 mm black & white—that's what I'd like. If it's not enough for both just get the Kodachrome. I have enough film for Japan but wanted some for my trip home—maybe I'll get to go by way of the Philippines or Hawaii, & I do want some for that. Since I'll be here for a couple of months, I think there will be time, so you won't have to hurry around. I told the mail clerk to have the M. O. made out to Mrs. Bell but it didn't come back that way so guess I'll have to take advantage of Dave's good nature.

What made me think of this today was because my replacement at the Bank came for an interview today & was accepted, I understand. For the first time it seemed so final that I was going to leave—was almost homesick for the old Bank already—guess I've just had my own way there too long 'cause they sure spoil me.

Wish you could peek in on my room tonight to see my Christmas card arrangement. I have 35 of them Scotch-taped on my wall around my dressing table. Looks a bit like a greeting card store, but I like it.

Must close; am in the middle of the best book, "The Fountainhead" & have to see how this chapter comes out.

Love,
Norma Jean

28 December

Hi!

Imagine me writing two days in a row! Ha!

Just thought of something I wanted to tell you. Mrs. Graf wrote & said she was sending a package to me at home in California, as she was uncertain about sending it to Tokyo until it was a little late. So if it comes, just keep it there as she said she thought it best that I wouldn't have to pack it up again. If you'd like to open it, it's all right with me—I realize how curious you can get about an unopened package.

It rained off & on all day again, but the sun shone a little this afternoon so think this storm's nearly over.

'Bye for now—I promise a longer note next time.

Love, N. J. jr.

Twenty-two

Dearest Mom & Dad,

Just realized I hadn't written you all year. Doesn't seem possible it could be 1949 already. Have surely been enjoying those snappy letters from home. I'm so glad you had such a nice Christmas & that Larry was able to be home. Dad—you were right on the ball this year with your price tags.

I had fun at New Year's. Only worked three days between Christmas & New Year's, & it really was a welcome vacation. New Year's Eve, Jack & I went to a party; then New Year's Day I went to eggnog open houses at Lt. Col. McComb's & Major Rose's. Sunday, I had the special New Year's Japanese food at Hamako-san's home. I was the only American & after dinner her mama-san, brother, two friends & I played cards. It was a riot—Mamasan was in rare form & had a gay time even though she was the loser in every game we played. Her house always fascinates me as it's down a dark, narrow alley, & up some dimly lighted narrow stairs. After you get in it's clean, well lit, fairly warm, & very neat. We had rice in every form imaginable—boiled, powdered, baked, toasted, in crackers, & cookies. Hamako had asked me if I liked zushi (raw fish), & when I showed no enthusiasm over it, she had eliminated it from the menu, for which I was certainly thankful. Once they get started with that, you find little pieces in everything served, & I always leave smelling like a fish & a slightly nauseated feeling every time I pass a fish market for a week afterward. When I left they gave me an armful of tangerines & rice cookies.

Scoop—have been trying to work it so I could take the Southern route home via either Guam or Manila & Hawaii & dock at San Francisco. Just got a phone call this morning from my "friend-o" & he said there's a ship leaving February 16th going that way that he will try to get me a reservation on. Am just keeping my fingers crossed.

I got the most scrumptious package from Larry. The See's candy he sent is really delicious. Everything was wrapped so cute & was in such good taste. My little Japanese typist gave me a lovely black lacquer candy bowl for New Year's. I got the cutest Christmas card from Sarah Kilgore from Arabia. She had her picture taken in an Arabian costume & put on the card. She said to come & join her & bring my own camel—love to go but haven't located the camel yet.

The lunch hour is up, & the typist needs the typewriter so best I quit holding up production.

All my love,
Norma Jean

9 January 1949

Dearest Esther,

Your last "8-pager" was really a masterpiece. Just loved hearing about your Christmas especially such a nice one as you had. I was so pleased the way Mother gave each of you some of the money I sent. She always does just the right thing it seems. Tell Dave to plan on wearing that jacket when I'm there—sounds real good.

Lois & I have been together a lot this week. It's so funny—we don't see each other for weeks then we have to catch up. I had lunch with her twice last week, went PXing Saturday together, went out with her & Bill & Bill's friend last night & am going to her house for dinner today. Her baby is due in about three months, & she's getting so anxious. We both wish I could be here then. She says she won't know how to take care of it & wanted my moral support. I told her all I could do would be read the directions from her baby book. She laughed, brought out the book, & we both went over some of the "do's & don'ts"—more fun.

Don't know whether you've read anything about it or not, but starting January 1st we're getting just 10% overseas differential instead of 25%. Anyone can go home, as this is contrary to the contracts we signed. An awful lot of civilians are going to. Sure am glad my contract is over. We will get free billeting but that's only $6 a month anyway.

Just paused to crack some nuts. Have more fun with them—bet the girls next door wonder what I keep pounding over here. Mary says she bets they think I'm hanging pictures all the time. She's really funny—keeps me in stitches. Takes Alka-Seltzer constantly, & the other day she asked if I thought she'd "sizzle-up" inside if she kept on taking so many. She has two big clocks on the shelf by her bed & they've never been right yet—she keeps checking on the time on the phone & my clock. She's from Boston & really has the accent. She's very easy going & keeps me laughing, so I'm lucky to have her with me.

Work at the Bank is very slow. The other afternoon we had nothing to do, so the Lt. tantalized us all by reading us recipes & showing us pictures of food from the "Woman's Home Companion". Were we ever hungry when the afternoon was over.

Must close & get ready to go to Lois' for dinner. She's having roast beef & cherry pie for dessert. Gad, here I go ending a letter talking about food again.

All my love,
Norma Jean

P.S. Your Christmas napkins & coasters are cute.

13 January 1949

Dearest Esther & Dave,

Hey, what's going on—snow in Southern California? Have been having to uphold "Sunny California" propaganda all day at the office. Golly, we haven't even had snow in Tokyo this year.

Another "What's going on"—what's the meaning of starting the year out on sick call, Dave? Was surely sorry to hear of your illness & sincerely hope they can get to the root of all this evil in a short time. I don't know about the Dr's. there, but I've seen some horrible looking skin ailments here that the Dr's. have cleared up in a very short time. Of course, it all depends on the kind you've got & I'm hoping yours is the easy-to-cure kind.

I haven't been doing anything too exciting. It's been nice to have more quiet evenings since the Holidays are over. Last night, I started to inventory my "loot"—what a job. It all looks like junk when I have to describe & price it. As usual, I didn't get too far. A couple of friends came to see me, then I had to stop & read letters, when I came to cleaning out some boxes.

I woke up this morning about 6 o'clock to the pitter–patter of several-hundred running feet. Who should it be racing by the Hotel but the local firemen—their black capes waving in the breezes. They ran down to the next block & did their morning exercises. Most are good acrobats & give shows once a year. Pretty soon the tired looking fire engines went "speeding" (about 5 mi. an hour) down the Avenue.

We are getting fresh milk now. Some company signed a contract for a recombining plant with the Govt. here; the milk is very good & tastes fresh. It's getting so civilized here now. Won't be able to tell about any rugged living when I get home. The Nips are really getting Westernized—even have pressure cookers for sale in their department stores.

Sure like the issue of the UCLA magazine I got today. It was good to see Bud's picture. I know so many people they mentioned, too. I always meant to write them a letter but never did.

Two Generals are coming to the Bank soon so we've been cleaning for two days. All we do is call a gang of Japanese laborers in & a G.I. tells them what to do. He's been having a gay time, & so far they've mopped five times, painted, brought fancy screens in, & varnished all our desks.

Let me know what it's like to see snow in California—that should be good. Did it hurt any of our trees at home? Will be thinking of you, Dave, & hope you're back on your feet real soon.

All my love,
Norma Jean

16 January 1949

Dearest Mom & Dad,

I'm glad we're friends, too. That was such a cute card. Your cheery letters & notes are always so welcome. Was glad to read Larry's letter, too. Snow in California really gets me. Bet the California weather jokes are really snowing you under.

I've had a nice weekend. Yesterday, I went to see the Japanese Sumo wrestlers, & it was sure interesting. I went to church this morning & PXing in the afternoon. Next weekend, I'm going to spend at the Fujiya Hotel at the base of Mt. Fuji. It's only about 80 miles from Tokyo so won't be a tiring trip. I've been there on Sundays but never for the weekend. It's supposed to be one of the most beautiful & is the most famous hotel so am looking forward to it. Am taking my bathing suit along as they have swimming pools & hot mineral baths.

I was sure sorry to hear Dave had to go to the hospital. Have been wondering how he's getting along. I hope they get to the cause real soon.

Mother, dear, how are you feeling? Do take good care of yourself. Hope those shots make you peppy real fast. Am sure glad you have regular check ups. I'm feeling fine. My iron pill appetite is still with me even though I haven't taken a pill for weeks. Our food has improved & everything tastes good again.

Am going to see "Carman" next week. It's going to be at the Imperial Theatre for allied personnel.

Haven't heard anything more about a definite shipping date. I've started filling out termination papers & have turned three in already, so I know things are going as they should. Everything I do has to go through Yokohama as I'm under 8th Army & not G.H.Q. as nearly everyone in Tokyo is.

I got a letter from Mrs. Graf last week. She said the funeral was followed by cremation. I was glad as I'd heard Emilie say that's what she thought was best, & I wondered if her parents knew that.

You should see me now—really it's lucky you can't I guess, as the room is really a mess. I felt ambitious this afternoon & cleaned out a lot of things. I have excelsior all over everything, clothes hanging on every available hook, boxes piled up, & my bed is high with odds & ends. Got tired of the mess myself so decided to visit with you awhile before putting things back together again. Even had the carpenter come up & put a hasp on my trunk as the lock broke. While he was doing that I was painting a box I had made for my slide projector so it really looked like a warehouse for awhile. It's a good thing Mary has a good disposition.

Best I quit so I can clean the place up—can't even go to bed until I do so 'bye for now.

All my love,
Norma Jean

P.S. Mrs. Graf said she received your letter & liked it so much. She said it was a little hard for her to write but wanted you to know she liked hearing from you.

25 January 1949

Dearest Mom & Dad,

Am just getting back into the old routine after my weekend in the mountains. I got the later train back Sunday evening & arrived in Tokyo about midnight, so I was pretty worn out yesterday. I really had a nice time, & it was so different from what I had expected on doing. I planned on having a real quiet, restful weekend. It started out fine. I walked out & took some pictures & came back to lunch Saturday morning. I was sitting there when the girl who had been assigned as my roommate joined me. We were having a fine time when another girl who I had come over with on the ship saw me & joined us. From then on, I kept meeting people I hadn't seen for months & was busy as a beaver catching up on news. The girl who was my roommate there, Kay, works for the Navy & some of her Navy friends came later on, so we all went to the dance Saturday night. They were Navy fliers & had just arrived from China the day before, so it was pretty interesting to hear the latest news from China first hand. Sunday we (about 5 had joined our little group by then) all went for a hike in the morning. It was a beautiful day; Fuji looked just like picture postcards. Although it didn't turn out the way I had planned, it was lots of fun, & it was nice to see my friends again.

Thanks a million for sending the money for my Social Workers "union" Mom. I really want to keep it up, as it will sure be a help to have it behind me. Will repay you shortly. Payday is next week & am a little low on cash at this point.

I got the prettiest package from Mrs. Graf yesterday. It was wrapped in silver paper with a huge red ribbon bow. Inside was a lovely box of stationery. She surely has been lovely to me.

Haven't heard anything more definite on my departure date. I called Eighth Army yesterday just to check. They have my papers in order but haven't booked me for a ship yet. I should get my orders before too long she said, so I know things are under control there.

Two generals came on a visit to our office yesterday. Haven't heard any repercussions yet so guess everything went along all right. They both seemed very nice. One came over after the introductions had been made & asked how things were going. He was the one who I had interviewed by in Yokohama when he was just a Colonel & I thought it was very nice of him. Work is certainly slow here now, & it makes the days seem rather long. I don't think the place will last too much longer because the work has really been finished. Just have to wait for the peace treaty now to decide who gets what. A lot of the offices here are about ready to fold up, & lots of jobs are being declared surplus. Sure glad my contract is up as things are rather unsettled all over. Just can't realize I've been here two years though.

I was glad to hear that Dave is getting along all right. Hope it is a permanent cure.

Esther sent two rolls of film, which really came in handy. Everyone over here seems to use that same size, & when they do get some it is all sold out before I can get a chance to get there.

Guess I've fooled around long enough. The conference is about to break up, & the wheels will be returning shortly, so best I go back to my desk. They don't care anymore now as we've kept asking for some work to do, & they couldn't give us any so they've become quite liberal about the whole thing. The fellow who's going to take my job over does most of my work now, so I don't have a chance.

Goodbye for now—more later when they have another conference.

Love,
Norma Jean

4 February 1949

Hi!

Bet I'm the happiest person in Japan! Just heard from 8th Army that my sailing date is the 16th. She said I will be on the USAT Gaffey, which will dock in San Francisco. Our phone connection was rather poor, so she wouldn't go into any detail. I'm supposed to go to Yokohama Monday to get orders for my hold baggage so will find out more then. Guess I really shouldn't tell you without knowing more details but golly, I am getting excited now.

Have been packing like mad—what a mess the room is. Am going to have an exciting weekend so will have a gay time 'til my last day here. Am going to Yokosuka, the Navy base, tomorrow. The Navy nurses have arranged for me to stay at their place. Will go to a dinner dance Saturday night there, then on a ride along the coast Sunday. Am going to the American Club for dinner tonight so must close & get ready.

More later.
Norma Jean

7 February, 1949

Dearest Family,

Just a note to keep you posted on the latest over here. They (8th Army) called my office this morning & said I was to sail Saturday, February 12th as the ship is arriving ahead of schedule. Soo—am I ever busy. I went to Yokohama to pick up my orders & have been packing fiendishly as it all has to be taken down at 9 o'clock tomorrow morning. There's a million details to take care of to get your clearance, & I have to make three more trips to Yokohama. The ship is scheduled to go via Hawaii, but I rather doubt that I'll get much time there as I think it's due in San Francisco in about two weeks after the departure date.

Jeepers—am I tired. I had such a wonderful weekend but a little strenuous. Saturday, I went to the dinner dance, & Sunday, we visited some tunnels with old Japanese Navy equipment still in them, then we went to the seaplane base & docks & went through Navy seaplanes & a Carrier ship.

Have so many people to say farewell to so will sure be madly rushing around. Am seeing Lois & Bill for dinner tomorrow.

One thing I wanted to tell you—don't get frightened if you receive a telegram as sometimes the Army will send ship-to-shore messages for you when you're 200 or 300 miles from shore, & it's fun to do I understand.

Just don't have time to do much writing, so please tell Esther & Larry about my plans for me.

Golly—hate to leave the place. The blossoms are just beginning & soon Japan will be in her most colorful season.

It's so sunny & warm during the day—just like spring.

I'm so darn tired & still a little more packing ahead of me so must close.

Mother darling, don't knock yourself out on anything—save the floors for me, huh?

Goodnight for now—
Norma Jean

11 February 1949

Dearest Mamasan & Papasan,

Have just finished sitting on the last suitcase to close it so am all set for sailing tomorrow. Boy, am I tired of packing! I would have come out okay, but I got several gifts that took lots of space so have had lots of problems making things fit. A sedan is going to pick me up at 8 o'clock tomorrow to take me to the dock. Ships usually always leave in the morning, but ours can't, as the Generals have to review their troops first (this should be good). So we sail at 1:30.

One thing I wanted to tell you—Jack works in communications & gets the ship's position daily. He said he would cable you when we had passed the date line & could give the estimated time of arrival. I thought it sounded good, as I'm not certain I can send a ship-to-shore message. You'll probably get several when we both work on it. Anyhow, if you get a cable from Jack Belrick about the arrival, don't be surprised. Esther said she might come to meet me in her last letter, so I thought best I let you know when I shall get there. These cables are free as the Army provides you to cable your home. Oh, yes, one other thing—I have to clear at the San Francisco Personnel office, & it may take a couple of days they tell me. Besides customs, we have to get our payroll clearance. I got my military scrip changed to greenbacks today, & it sure looked funny again. I went out & spent all the yen I had—more fun. Got my medical clearance this afternoon, & thank heaven they didn't give me any more shots.

This is my last night in old Tokyo, & I know I'll really miss the place. Always hated "goodbyes" & if it weren't for such a wonderful family on the other side of the Pacific I suppose I'd just stay on & on rather than say farewell to Japan & my friends here. Have written to the Grafs, so they know I'm leaving also. Must close & give the Japanese sandman one last job. Goodnight my dears, see you shortly.

All my love,
Norma Jean

Earle Kirkbride

WESTERN UNION

DA001 SPD49

D.SFA540 INTL FR=SF USAT GENERALGAFFEY VIA MACKAY RADIO

13 21 2218 GMT=

MR NORMAN CONE=

310 WEST LAUREL ST COMPTON CALIF=

ARRIVE FORT MASON FEBRUARY 24[TH]=

Epilogue

Thus ended the first overseas assignment for Norma Jean Cone. After working as a registered social worker in southern California for a few months, Jean began a career in recreation for the U.S. military. Her first assignment, starting in 1950, was in the Philippines for the Air Force. While there, she had considerable contact with her cousin Erwin Ross at the U.S. Consulate, and she traveled to South Korea to open service clubs for the Air Force.

Following her tour in the Philippines, Jean was located in England until late 1957. During this period she dealt with service clubs primarily in northern Europe and continued to write interesting letters home.